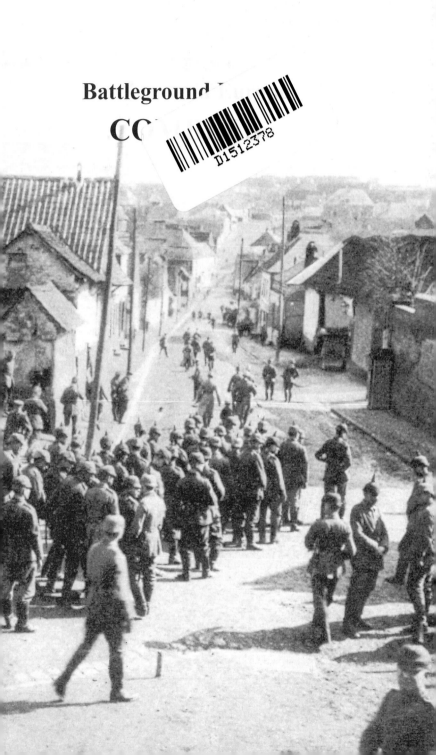

Battleground

CO

Battleground Europe
COMBLES

Paul Reed

Series editor
Nigel Cave

LEO COOPER

First published in 2002 by
LEO COOPER
an imprint of
Pen & Sword Books Limited
47 Church Street, Barnsley, South Yorkshire S70 2AS

ISBN 0 85052 674 4

A CIP catalogue record of this book is available
from the British Library

Printed by CPI UK

*For up-to-date information on other titles produced under the Leo Cooper imprint,
please telephone or write to:*

Pen & Sword Books Ltd, FREEPOST, 47 Church Street
Barnsley, South Yorkshire S70 2AS
Telephone 01226 734222

CONTENTS

Introduction by Series Editor

The large village of Combles is on the extreme left, southernmost part, of the British advance on the Somme during the summer and autumn days of 1916. It is an area that is very rarely visited by the numerous British pilgrims and tourists to the battlefields, and this book provides a welcome opportunity to encourage more to come to what is a fascinating area. It is not as though some of the features in and around Combles are not generally well covered in various Great War classics - the catacombs in Combles itself; the infamous 'Lousy' Wood; Falfemont Farm; Bouleux Wood; and the well-known cross of Major Cedric Dickens. It also serves to bring the visitor close to the French sector of the Somme - our allies who had borne the brunt of the fighting for the first two years of the war and whose role in the conflict we British too often tend to undervalue. The cemeteries mentioned in this book do not have the great streams of visitors that some, especially in the northern sector, receive, and it is to be hoped that time will be given to walk amongst the headstones of the fallen British, French and German soldiers buried in them.

Paul Reed rightly concentrates much of the book on the exploits of the 56th (London) Division, and there is a very useful outline explanation of that highly unusual body of infantry, the London Regiment. But my first introduction to the area came in reading the life of Father William Doyle SJ, MC, a chaplain in the 16th (Irish) Division, who found himself there in the period following the fall of the neighbouring village of Guillemont in the early days of September 1916. In his letters to his father he portrays something of the nightmare that was involved in operations.

He describes the march up to hold the line in the area of Leuze Wood:

> *The first part of our journey lay through a narrow trench, the floor of which consisted of deep, thick mud, and the bodies of dead men trodden under foot. It was horrible beyond description, but there was no help for it, and on the half-rotten corpses of our own brave men we marched in silence, everyone busy with his own thoughts. I shall spare you gruesome details, but you can picture one's sensations as one felt the ground yield under one's foot, and one sank through the body of some poor fellow.*

Eventually they moved out into the open, coming onto the scene of recent very heavy fighting.

> *The wounded, at least I hope so, had all been removed, but*

the dead lay there stiff and stark, with open, staring eyes, just as they had fallen. Good God, such a sight! I had tried to prepare myself for this, but all I had read or pictured gave me very little idea of the reality. Some lay as if they were sleeping quietly, others had died in agony, or had had the life crushed out of them by mortal fear, while the whole ground, every foot of it, was littered with heads or limbs, or pieces of torn human bodies.
They came to a sunken road.

'Here the retreating Germans had evidently made a last desperate stand, but had been caught by our artillery fire. The dead lay in piles, the blue grey uniforms broken by many a khaki-clad body. I saw the ruins of what was evidently the dressing station, judging by the number of bandaged men about; but a shell had found them out even here and swept them all into the net of death.'

The inexorable effect of time means that we have hardly any of those who fought here left. We have the photographs, of course - but they are in black and white, and one veteran I spoke to made a telling (if, on reflection, obvious) point that they saw it in colour - the whole, awesome, gruesome spectacle. We can have no concept of the sounds of passing bullets and the crash of shell, the screams and the stench; we can have no idea of the richness of comradeship forged in war and yet the cheapness of life. Now we are dependent on imagination and the recorded memories of those who fought and endured here.

It is to be hoped that books such as this will help to bring into sharper focus these memories; and to help us to respect the men who came from all over Europe (and beyond) to fight in this quiet 'corner of a foreign field'.

Nigel Cave,
Porta Latina, Rome

Introduction

Combles is one of those locations on the Somme battlefield that does not immediately attract the attention of the average visitor to the area. Indeed, few will have heard of it, or be aware of either its location or importance in the battle. The benefit of a series like **Battleground Europe** is that the many corners of the 'forgotten Somme', a world away from sites like the Newfoundland Park and Thiepval, are finally brought to the attention of the reader and battlefield visitor. And as with *Courcelette*, I am grateful to Pen & Sword for giving me the opportunity to tell the story of what happened there.

In 1916 Combles was one of the largest villages on the Somme. It was flanked by two important woods, Bouleaux Wood and Leuze Wood, which themselves dominated the ground towards Guillemont and Ginchy. Falfemont Farm and Wedge Wood guarded the southern approaches, and in September 1916 there was nearly four weeks of furious fighting for this tiny corner of Picardy.

The operations at Combles involved largely the units of the 56th (1st London) Division. This territorial formation has long been an interest of mine, together with its sister London divisions: 47th, 58th and 60th. The readers of many recent books on the war might be forgiven for thinking sometimes that the northern Pals battalions, who indeed fell in such great numbers on the Somme in 1916, were the only British army units involved in the battle. The activities of the London Regiment are largely forgotten, and having had the privilege of knowing a large number of '56th Men', I had felt for a long time that part of their story had to be told – and here it is with *Combles*.

With the passing of the eighty-fifth anniversary of the Battle of the Somme, for the first time perhaps we saw it without the company of a veteran. The eleventh hour for the men of that war has long since passed, and some of those that I interviewed as a boy have been dead more than twenty years. How will our understanding of the Somme, of the war as a whole, be different now that we have no-one to ask if what we write sounds like half the truth of what really happened?

Many of the men I knew earnestly believed the war would be forgotten once they were dead. I hope their spirits can now look down in wonder at the hundreds of thousands of visitors the old battlefields receive each year – with the number ever growing. And I hope that such visitors will remember that the Somme lasted longer than just one day, that Ypres wasn't all mud and Passchendaele, and that the soldiers of the BEF pulled off some of the greatest feats of arms ever performed by British soldiers. And I equally hope that the day will come when I don't gaze out across battlefields like those at Combles, seeing the coaches and the cars pass me, each one with the familiar GB sticker, and ask my old comrades if it isn't better that these visitors are unwise to the real truth?

Paul Reed
Sussex & The Somme
January 2002

battlefields1418@hotmail.com

Acknowledgements

Having had an interest in the London Regiment for a long time, there are many with whom I have exchanged ideas and research over the years. Some of them were part of that infamous group of London Regiment medal collectors who, through preserving the medals and documents associated with many London lads, have 'kept the memory green', often over a pint in the bar of the yearly OMRS Convention or the canteen at the PRO! Among the 'London Mob' I'd especially like to thank are: Roni Bhairman, Steve Brookes, Mick de Caville, Bob Crane, John Eagle, Dave Halsey, Steve Knight, Andy McKinnon, Paul Morrissey, Tony & Joan Poucher, Peter Wardrop and the late Jack Stratful.

Special thanks goes to Combles veteran, the late Harry Coates, who served in the London Scottish and latterly on the Brigade staff. I spent many interesting hours talking to Harry, and learnt a lot from him.

Major Tony Swift kindly supplied the details of his uncle, L/Cpl H.Woodfield, who was killed at Leuze Wood in September 1916.

This is the first book I have written where the CD ROM *Soldiers Died in the Great War* has proved to be a key research tool. This excellent inter-active database has enabled me to trace many soldiers where only a surname was listed in the regimental records, and has proved very useful in finalising casualties for many of the battalions. As such I can thoroughly recommend it to all Great War authors and researchers. My thanks to the Naval & Military Press for making it available. Further details can be found on their web site at: http://www.great-war-casualties.com/

The official photographs are reproduced courtesy of the Imperial War Museum, London. Mr Ian Carter of the Photographic Archive was extremely helpful in this respect. All other photographs are from the author's archives, unless otherwise credited.

In France I would like to thank: Tom & Janet Fairgrieve of Delville Wood, Peter Franks, Jean-Pierre Matte of Bernafay Wood, Douglas Meney, Vic & Diane Piuk and Peter & Sarah Wright.

At Pen & Sword, Charles Hewitt is always helpful and supportive, and I once more extend my thanks to the 'back room boys' Roni, Paul and Jon Wilkinson for their help, advice and good humour when it finally comes to putting the books together.

Finally, my love and thanks to Kieron, Edmund and Poppy. What will our children make of an early life spent trudging the open Picardy fields and wandering around cemeteries?

Advice to Travellers

The Somme remains one of the most visited battlefields on the old Western Front, and as the years pass, more and more facilities are available. Accommodation poses few problems as there are now many hotels, gites and the more favoured 'chambre d'hote' establishments, often run by British couples. In Combles itself the only available accommodation is a house for rent, owned by a retired Englishman. For further details contact Peter Franks on (01922) 642805.

The nearest B&B to Combles is:

'Les Alouettes', 10 Rue du Mantier, 80360 Hardecourt-aux-Bois, France.

Contact: Tel/Fax - 0033 3.22.85.14.56.

or email: PVSkylark@aol.com.

Here an English couple, Vic and Diane Piuk, have three rooms available, all of which have en-suite facilities. Both breakfast and evening meals are available. Vic and Diane also have use of a self-catering chalet for rent, which is located not far from their house and bookings can be made through them.

Not far away is:

Bernafay Wood Bed & Breakfast, 55 Grande Rue, 80330 Montauban-en-Picardie, France.

Contact: Tel/Fax – 0033 3.22.85.02.47.

or email: bernafaywood@aol.com.

Here Monsieur Jean-Pierre Matte, a local Great War expert, runs an excellent B&B with his wife Christine in the heart of the famous Bernafay Wood. It is located in the old railway station buildings, and there are five rooms, with en-suite facilities for most of them. Breakfast is provided and there is a small kitchen to cook your own meals in the evening, if desired. English is spoken.

Hotels in Albert are few, and many English visitors favour the Hotel de la Paix, now run by the friendly and hospitable Mme Isabelle Daudigny. Tel: 0033.3.22.75.01.64. But there are others, and information on them can be found in the Tourist Information Office in Albert, opposite the basilica. Battlefield accommodation can also be found on the WFA website at: www.western-front.com and the Somme Tourist Board web site at: www.anzac.org.

There are two main museums on the Somme. At Peronne the Historial de la Grande Guerre offers a modern approach where objects are few and visitors are directed towards interpretation rather than fact. In Albert the Musee des Abris, amid the tunnels below the town, has an interesting array of Great War artefacts on display, arranged among life size dioramas of trenches and dugouts. It is well backed up with photographs and maps, and there is a good shop selling battlefield relics and books. The visitor's centre at Delville Wood offers the greatest selection of material, and the whole **Battleground Europe** series is on sale here. All these places operate varying open times between the summer and winter seasons, and Delville Wood is always closed on a Monday.

Weather can be unpredictable on the Somme, and it is best to prepare for extremities of heat and cold. In the summer months a hat gives protection from the sun which beats down on fields devoid of cover. Water and sun cream are usefully carried in a small pack with all your other essential gear. In the winter always have a jumper and waterproofs at hand, and if walking the ground a good pair of boots.

Combles, unlike most Somme villages, boasts a number of cafés and shops. The opening times of these will vary, and not follow the sort of hours most English visitors are used to back home. Nearby in Longueval is the Café Calypso, which is normally open for drinks at all hours and usually can muster up some lunch. The owner, Monsieur Jean Blondell, is also the mayor and heartily welcomes British visitors.

As with anywhere on the battlefields respect the rights and privacy of the locals who own the land. Both Leuze and Bouleaux Woods are not open to the public, and metal detecting or digging in them is most unwelcome, and may result in a visit to the Combles gendarmerie, who frown on such activities. Walking in and around them with this book, or some trench maps, will be better understood, although be prepared to leave if asked to do so by the gamekeeper. During the shooting season (late September onwards) it is unwise to walk in any wood, as French hunters abound with the intent of shooting anything that moves.

For those with more than a passing interest in the Great War, membership of the Western Front Association is essential. Founded by John Giles in 1980, the WFA now has branches all over the United Kingdom, and indeed overseas – some of which meet on a monthly basis. The annual subscription includes copies of the in-house newsletter, *The Bulletin*, and the glossy magazine, *Stand To!* Members also have access to the WFA's collection of trench maps and cheap photocopies are available – including several of Combles. For further details contact:

> The Western Front Association
> PO BOX 1914
> Reading
> Berkshire
> RG4 7YP

Chapter One

THE ROAD TO COMBLES

Combles, one of the largest villages on the Somme, fell to men of the 56th (London) Division on 26 September 1916 following several weeks of intensive fighting. As the chief protagonists in this battle were mainly men of the London Regiment, it is worthwhile beginning this account with a brief look at that regiment and how it came into being. Under German occupation for nearly two years, we will also examine the town's role as a billet for German troops, and then look at the events leading up to the fighting around Combles, which was prefaced by the capture of Falfemont Farm.

London Town to the Somme: The London Regiment 1908-1916

The British Army prior to the Great War was different from most European armies in that it was comprised entirely of volunteers. Long

Soldiers of the 14th London Regiment (London Scottish) parade at Dorking in 1914. They have been issued with 1914 Pattern Leather equipment and Long Lee Enfields.

gone were the press-gangs and conscription was unknown in Britain. Because of this it was also a lot smaller than most of its European contemporaries, the British Army by May 1914 only numbering 250,000 men, compared to a potential five million in the German Army when fully mobilised. To supplement this, the British had a long experience of militia and volunteer units. The descendants of these were formalised in the army reforms of 1908 by the formation of the Territorial Force (TF) – part-time reserve units of infantry, cavalry and artillery, with various support units. Each county regiment formed one or more of these TF Bns, but in certain counties no regular regiment existed and special TF ones were formed in their place. This was the case in London.

The London Regiment was the largest territorial regiment in the British Army, with twenty-six battalions by 1914. Formed from the old Volunteer Companies in April 1908, each battalion was affiliated to a regular army regiment, following that unit's traditions and military dress. For example the 9th Battalion (Queen Victoria's Rifles) were affiliated to the King's Royal Rifle Corps, and being a rifle regiment wore blackened buttons and shoulder titles, and referred to bayonets as 'swords'. Indeed, in contemporary records of the 9th Londons, the rank of private is often substituted with 'rifleman'.

Being recruits into what was then called the Territorial Force, and after the Great War, the Territorial Army, the men of the London Regiment were not full-time soldiers. They joined their battalion on a regular basis, attending evening drill sessions, weekend camps and a large annual camp when the battalion went on manoeuvres, often with other London battalions. Attendance at all these was compulsory, if the recruit was to enjoy the pay he received in return for his services. He also joined on for periods of four years, and could not break free from this commitment unless discharged due to ill health or misconduct, or by buying himself out.

Battalions also recruited on a local basis, each one having their own drill-hall cum headquarters in their local district. This effectively made them locally-raised units, where men from the same district of London, often living in the same street, working in the same factory, railway station or docks, having attended the same school, football club or church all joined and served together. As such they took on distinct local identities, some of which were formalised in their unit title. Although the battalions were each numbered from one to twenty-eight (the 26th and 27th Bns never being formed), they often had a title by which they were better known – some being unofficial titles.

The full list is:

1st Bn	(Royal Fusiliers)
2nd Bn	(Royal Fusiliers)
3rd Bn	(Royal Fusiliers)
4th Bn	(Royal Fusiliers)
5th Bn	(London Rifle Brigade)
6th Bn	(Cast Iron Sixth)
7th Bn	(Shiny Seventh)
8th Bn	(Post Office Rifles)
9th Bn	(Queen Victoria's Rifles)
10th Bn	(Hackney)
11th Bn	(Finsbury)
12th Bn	(The Rangers)
13th Bn	(Kensingtons)
14th Bn	(London Scottish)
15th Bn	(Civil Service Rifles)
16th Bn	(Queen's Westminster Rifles)
17th Bn	(Poplar & Stepney)
18th Bn	(London Irish Rifles)
19th Bn	(St Pancras)
20th Bn	(Blackheath & Woolwich)
21st Bn	(First Surrey Rifles)
22nd Bn	(Queen's)
23rd Bn	(Queen's)
24th Bn	(Queen's)
25th Bn	(Cyclists)
28th Bn	(Artist's Rifles)

For most London battalions it did not cost the recruit any money to join the battalion, indeed the battalion paid him for his time and services. This was an obvious attraction to many working-class London men, particularly in a period when unemployment was high. Some battalions, wishing to retain an exclusivity among its members, therefore demanded a joining fee (sometimes as much as £10) – thus deterring any working class enlistees. Among units to do this were the London Scottish, Queen's Westminster Rifles and the London Rifle Brigade. The introduction of such a scheme further perpetuated the exclusivity of these units as it gave them funds to become amongst the best-equipped battalions in the whole Territorial Force. For example the London Scottish was the only unit to have two Vickers machine-guns by 1914, rather than the inferior issue Maxim guns.

56th (London) Division Lewis Gun course, somewhere in France. The officer is from the London Scottish and the others from a wide mix of units in the Division.

All these factors affected recruitment, and the eventual size of each London battalion. The full peacetime establishment of an infantry battalion was roughly 1,100 men – few London Regiment battalions matched this figure by the summer of 1914. Indeed, in some the establishment was as low as 400 men. It was no coincidence that those with the lower establishment were battalions like the 10th (Hackney), recruited in working-class districts.[1]

Another factor in the life of a London TF recruit, no matter which battalion he was in, was the vexed subject of Imperial Service. No territorial soldier could be sent outside of Great Britain without having volunteered to do so under the Imperial Service scheme. To do so meant more money, but records seem to indicate that the number of men volunteering for Imperial Service was low generally throughout the Territorial Force. Perhaps many of them saw it as a safe job? However, in some units it was expected that when you joined, you

immediately signed up for Imperial Service. Records show that it was largely the well-equipped, fee-paying, class-ridden battalions of the London Regiment that had signed up for this duty in large numbers, so that when war came in August 1914, it was no surprise that the War Office chose these men to spearhead the use of territorial units in a European conflict.

When war did come, the War Office had mixed feelings about using territorials in the fighting zone. Most senior officers saw them as useful garrison troops to free-up regular battalions stationed in Britain, or for fetching and carrying on the Lines of Communication. Indeed, a number of London Regiments were mobilised as early as August 1914 and despatched to France the following month – only to find themselves involved in such duties. However, once the regular units of the British Expeditionary Force (BEF) met their German opposition in France and Flanders losses began to mount. Lord Kitchener, Secretary of State for War, realised that a conflict which his political colleagues had promised would be over 'by Christmas' would now be a protracted affair. As such he appealed for 100,000 war volunteers and released the Territorial Force for service as front-line units.

For the London Regiment this first taste of combat came on Halloween 1914, when on the 31st October the London Scottish fought what became a very famous action at Messines in Flanders. They gained the honour of not only being the first London regiment battalion to come under fire, but the first infantry battalion in the whole Territorial Force to do so. By this time there were about another dozen London battalions in France, and these were released from Lines of Communications and joined regular army Divisions in the field. Some lost men from shell-fire or snipers, but by November 1914 the first phase of fighting had ended and trench warfare begun.

Throughout the first half of 1915 several London battalions fought alongside regular units in a number of different divisions. They fought in various battles from Neuve-Chapelle to Aubers Ridge and Festubert. Meanwhile in England, other London battalions were being grouped into their own divisions – their pre-war establishments being increased by the influx of wartime volunteers. The first complete one, the 47th (London) Division, landed in France just in time to take a minor part in the battle of Festubert in May 1915. Four months later it fought at Loos, when the first significant losses to be sustained by the regiment were incurred. In early 1916 the remaining London battalions which were still attached to regular divisions were finally grouped together into their own formation – the 56th (London) Division. Two Middlesex TF battalions were added to one brigade to make up the requisite twelve battalions for the Division. The order of battle was:

167th Brigade:
1/1st Bn London Regiment
1/3rd Bn London Regiment
1/7th Bn Middlesex Regiment
1/8th Bn Middlesex Regiment
168th Brigade:
1/4th Bn London Regiment
1/12th Bn London Regiment
1/13th Bn London Regiment
1/14th Bn London Regiment
169th Brigade:
1/2nd Bn London Regiment
1/5th Bn London Regiment
1/9th Bn London Regiment
1/16th Bn London Regiment

The **167th Brigade** consisted of the following battalions:

1/1st Bn London Regiment (Royal Fusiliers): 1st London Regiment was one of four in the regiment to be affiliated with the Royal Fusiliers. They all wore a similar cap badge (the flaming grenade) and adhered to the traditions of their parent regiment. Their Drill Hall was located at Handel Street in Bloomsbury and they were part of the original 1st London Division when war broke out. In September 1914 they were posted to Malta as garrison troops until February 1915 when they came back to England, before moving to France in March. Here the now 1/1st Bn joined 25th Brigade, 8th Division, and served in the line south of Armentières until it eventually joined 56th (London) Division. At the Battle of Aubers Ridge on 9 May, however, it took part in the assault, losing 3 officers and 120 men.

1/3rd Bn London Regiment (Royal Fusiliers): 3rd London Regiment was another of the Fusilier battalions, but its Drill Hall was at Edward Street in Hampstead Road, West London. Another original 1st London Division unit, it was likewise sent on garrison duty in Malta, but was transferred to France in January 1915, crossing via Marseilles. South of Armentières the now 1/3rd joined the Garwhal Brigade of the Meerut Division, Indian Army Corps, and was one of the leading battalions in the Battle of Neuve Chapelle on 10th March 1915. As such it was the second London unit to see action in the Great War. Total casualties in this operation were 8 officers and 160 men. Remaining in this sector until November, the 1/3rd joined 139th Brigade, 46th (North Midland) Division on the Ypres front. Two weeks later it moved to 142nd Brigade, 47th (2nd London) Division, in the Loos area. Here it stayed until the formation of the new division.

1/7th Bn Middlesex Regiment: The 7th Middlesex were a pre-war TF battalion, one of four in the Middlesex Regiment. Its Drill Hall was at Priory Road, Hornsea and when war broke out was part of the Middlesex Brigade of the Home Counties Division. Being virtually at full strength, something that was fairly rare in a county regiment TF unit, it was selected as one of several territorial battalions to go out to Gibraltar to relieve regular army troops for France, in September 1914. Here it was to remain until February 1915, when it returned to England via Avonmouth. Within a month the now 1/7th Bn (several reserve battalions having been formed in the meantime) was despatched to France, landing at Le Havre on 13th March. Here it joined 23rd Brigade of 8th Division, a regular army formation, the battalion strength being 31 officers and 904 other ranks. During the Battle of Aubers Ridge the 1/7th were in reserve, and because of their relatively light casualties during this period, the unit was dubbed 'The Lucky Seventh'. It remained in the area south of Armentières until joining the 56th (London) Division in 1916.

1/8th Bn Middlesex Regiment: Like the 7th, the 8th was also a pre-war TF battalion and its Drill Hall located at Hanworth Road in Hounslow. Part of the same Middlesex Brigade, it accompanied the 7th to Gibraltar while back in England several reserve battalions were formed and it now became designated as 1/8th Middlesex. In February 1915 it returned to England, and while waiting to embark at Gibraltar the 2/8th was disembarking at the same time. It was the only time during the Great War when both battalions met up. The 1/8th crossed to France via Le Havre on 9th March 1915, and proceeded to join 85th Brigade, 28th Division, which also contained the 3rd Middlesex, a regular unit. Here it underwent training and in April served in the line during the Second Battle of Ypres. It was heavily gassed at Zonnebeke, and suffered severe losses. By 30th May, the battalion was down to a strength of just below 400 men. On 21st June the 1/8th were transferred to the 8th Division and amalgamated with the 1/7th until reinforcements from the 3/8th in England arrived towards the end of the year, after which it joined the 56th (London) Division.

The 168th Brigade consisted of the following battalions:

1/4th Bn London Regiment (Royal Fusiliers): The last of the Fusilier battalions, 4th Londons had their Drill Hall at Shaftesbury Street on the City Road in North London. An original 1st London Division unit, the 4th were on guard duty along the railway line between Waterloo and Basingstoke when war broke out. Posted to Malta on garrison duties, the now 1/4th crossed to France via Marseilles in January 1915, joining the Ferozepore Brigade, Lahore Division, Indian Corps. It was in reserve for Neuve Chapelle, and moved to the Ypres Salient in April where it took part in the fighting near Buffs Road and Oblong Farm. Here it lost nearly 200 officers and men. Returning to the trenches south of Armentières in May, the 1/4th accompanied the 1/3rd Londons to 46th (North Midland) and then 47th (2nd London) Divisions in November. The battalion stayed in the Loos area until the new division was formed in 1916.

1/12th Bn London Regiment (Rangers): An original 1st London Division unit, the Rangers were one of many London battalions affiliated to the King's Royal Rifle Corps, wearing black buttons and shoulder titles and referring to the bayonet as a sword, as is common in rifle regiments. Its Drill Hall was in Chenies Street, Bedford Square, and tended to attract a high proportion of Middle Class men into its ranks before the war. At virtually full strength in August 1914, and with a large number of men who had elected for Imperial Service, it crossed to France via Le Havre on Christmas Day 1914. Here it became Lines of Communication troops in the Ypres area and then joined 84th Brigade, 28th Division in February 1915. The now 1/12th (Rangers) took part in the fighting for Hill 60 and then Second Ypres in April-May on the Frezenberg Ridge, where it had heavy losses. A composite battalion was formed with the LRB and Kensingtons, when the Rangers became GHQ troops until the re-formation of the 1st London Division in 1916. By this time many of the original members of the unit, because of their social background, had been commissioned and the ranks were reinforced with recruits from the 2/12th and 3/12th battalions in England.

1/13th Bn London Regiment (Kensingtons): A proud and perhaps socially elite battalion, the 13th Londons had their Drill Hall at Iverna Gardens in Kensington. Many well known families of this part of London were represented among the officers and men in this unit, which included the war artist Eric Kennington and the grandson of the author Charles Dickens, Cedric Dickens. Being at full strength and with a high proportion of Imperial Service men, it was no accident that it was amongst the first of the London battalions to land in France in November 1914. Here it joined the 25th Brigade, 8th Division, south of Armentières and took part in the Battle of Neuve Chapelle in March 1915, with 156 casualties. The Kensingtons were especially selected by Brigadier General A.W.G.L.Cole CB DSO, commanding 25th Brigade, for Aubers Ridge on 9th May. He is reputed to have said, 'they will not fail me'. In this operation losses amounted to 13 officers and 423 other ranks, and afterwards the battalion was transferred to Lines of Communication until February 1916 when they joined the 56th (London) Division. By this time reinforcements from the 2/13th and 3/13th had arrived from England.

1/14th Bn London Regiment (London Scottish): Arguably the most famous of all the London battalions, the London Scottish were affiliated to the Gordon Highlanders and had their Drill Hall next door to the QWR at 59 Buckingham Gate, Westminster. They operated a very strict enlistment procedure before the war. Indeed, a recruit was not only required to prove Scottish heritage to join the 'London Jocks', he also had to pay for the privilege! As such it created a socially elite battalion, from which the largest number of commissions in a single London battalion were drawn from among the ranks. When war broke out the London Scottish were on their annual camp and at full strength with almost every man signed up for Imperial Service. As such it was the first London Regiment battalion to cross to France in September 1914, and indeed one of the first in the whole TF. Initially it was posted to GHQ troops, but in late October was attached to the Cavalry Corps and took part in the fighting at Messines on 31st October: being the first territorial infantry battalion to see action in the Great War. The following month it was posted to 1st Brigade, 1st Division and transferred to the La Bassée Canal sector in early 1915. It was in support for the Battle of Aubers Ridge on 9th May, and then moved to the Vermelles area. In the Battle of Loos it attacked the area around Lone Tree on 25th September, suffering heavy casualties. The London Scottish remained in the Loos sector until the 56th (London) Division was created.

The 169th Brigade consisted of the following battalions:

1/2nd Bn London Regiment (Royal Fusiliers): The 2nd Londons were a Royal Fusilier affiliated battalion whose Drill Hall was located at Tufton Street, Westminster. An original 1st London Division unit, it was guarding the railway lines near Southampton Docks when war was declared. Like the other Fusilier battalions it went to the Malta garrison in September 1914, and came via Marseilles to the Western Front in January 1915. Here the now 1/2nd Londons joined 17th Brigade, 6th Division, in the line east of Armentières until June, when they moved to the Ypres Salient. It served in the fighting for Hooge in August, and in the line near Sanctuary Wood and Zillebeke. In October the 17th Brigade was transferred to the 24th Division on the Messines Ridge, and it was from here that the 1/2nd moved to join the 56th (London) Division in February 1916.

1/5th Bn London Regiment (London Rifle Brigade): The LRB were affiliated to the Rifle Brigade, and wore black buttons and shoulder titles. Its Drill Hall was at Bunhill Row, and the battalions was on annual camp at Crowborough in Sussex when war broke out. The LRB was another of the socially elite battalions of the London Regiment, and its ranks included many Middle Class men at this time – among them the author Henry Williamson. At virtually full strength in August 1914, it also had a high number of Imperial Service men and as such crossed to France in November 1914, proceeding to the Ypres front. Here it joined 11th Brigade, 4th Division, and spent the winter of 1914/15 in the 'Plugstreet Wood' area. During Second Ypres the now 1/5th battalion was at Wieltje in April-May and lost 16 officers and 392 other ranks in the fighting here. Lance Sergeant D.W.Belcher of the LRB was awarded the Victoria Cross for bravery near Wieltje at this time. Due to the heavy losses, the LRB became GHQ troops and formed a composite unit with the Rangers and the Kensingtons. In August 1915 the LRB joined 8th Brigade, 3rd Division, at Ypres until

Typical wartime recruit into the 5th Londons (London Rifle Brigade) showing the cloth shoulder title that was worn from late 1914.

the formation of the 56th (London) Division in 1916.

   1/9th Bn London Regiment (Queen Victoria's Rifles): The QVRs had their Drill Hall at 56 Davies Street, near Berkeley Square, and were affiliated to the King's Royal Rifles Corps, wearing the usual black buttons and shoulder titles. When war broke out they were at their annual camp near Pirbright. Another of the London battalions that was largely made up of Middle Class men, at full strength and with a high proportion of Imperial Service recruits, the QVRs crossed to France in November 1914. Here they moved up to Ypres and joined 13th Brigade, 5th Division. During Second Ypres in April 1915, the battalion was in the defence of Hill 60 and Second Lieutenant Harold Wooley was awarded the Victoria Cross for his bravery here. He became the first London Regiment soldier, and the first Territorial officer, to win the VC in the Great War. In the summer of 1915 the QVRs went south to the Somme, and took over the trenches near Carnoy. They moved from the Somme to join the 56th (London) Division in February 1916.

1/16th Bn London Regiment (Queen's Westminster Rifles): The Queen's Westminster's had their Drill Hall next door to the London Scottish at Buckingham Gate in Westminster. They were at Hemel Hempstead in August 1914, and were another of the socially elite battalions with a good recruiting record. The QWR crossed to France in November 1914 to join 18th Brigade, 6th Division. Here they served in the Houplines sector east of Armentières and then in the Ypres Salient. They were to remain in the Ypres area until the formation of the 56th (London) Division, and personnel from this unit assisted Rev. P.S.B. 'Tubby' Clayton to establish Talbot House at Poperinghe in 1915.

The division's Support Units came from a wide variety of backgrounds and experience. The artillery were part of the 1st London Division's original allocation, comprising three TF brigades, the 1/1st, 1/2nd and 1/3rd London Brigades Royal Field Artillery (RFA). In addition, the 1/4th London Howitzer Brigade RFA and 56th Divisional

Ammunition Column also formed part of the artillery allocation, the latter being formed from TF personnel in the other RFA units. Two London TF Field Companies of the Royal Engineers (later numbered 512th and 513th) were joined by the 416th (Edinburgh) Field Company, which had seen previous service on the Western Front. Stokes mortar batteries, one per brigade, were formed from infantry and RFA personnel from a mix of units, and the Brigade Machine Gun Companies of the Machine Gun Corps (numbered 167th, 168th and 169th) were drawn from the old machine-gun sections in the four infantry battalions of each brigade. Thus they retained a 'London' feel to them, until unit casualties were replaced from the Somme fighting onwards. The 1/5th Battalion of the Cheshire Regiment joined the 56th and became the divisional Pioneer Battalion, the only non-London Regiment unit in the division.

This was the division which would eventually fight for and take Combles in September 1916, and we shall therefore return to it later.

Combles Under German Occupation

The often forgotten fighting on the Somme in 1914 largely passed Combles by. The German army, steamrollering across Picardy, were finally opposed by the French on the Somme in early September 1914. Near Combles actions took place at Ginchy and Flers involving the French 82nd Territorial Division, and others at Guillemont and Le Transloy. Combles was swept up without a fight – ironically two years later, the village would fall to the Germans once more – and again without a fight. Following this capture of Combles and the surrounding area, the front lines were established to the west, between Montauban,

Happier days. The peaceful village of Combles, soon to be ravaged by war.

The streets of Combles filled with Germans after it had been taken without a fight.

Maricourt and Hardecourt-aux-Bois – and beyond that to the south-west to Maurepas and the Somme river valley. These front lines, at first occupied by the French, were handed over to the British in the autumn of 1915, when the trenches at Maricourt became the 'right of the line' on the British sector of the Western Front. Here the lines joined with their French allies opposite Hardecourt.

Combles was a large village in 1914: with a big town hall, a brick factory, railway station and several imposing houses. One, owned by Monsieur Proyart, was a second home – he also had a chateau in the nearby village of Courcelette. He was to lose both in the destruction wrought by the Great War. To the west Combles was flanked by two areas of woodland. Leuze Wood, south of the Combles – Guillemont road, was the larger of the two, and the long, narrow Bouleaux Wood which was situated on the opposite, north side, of the same road. The whole village sat in a hollow, and these woods gave further shelter from observation from the front line positions between Montauban and Hardecourt, making Combles a 'safe' area in the German lines.

To the south-west the ground rose over huge open fields, cut only

The church in Combles prior to the British bombardment.

The ruins of Combles church, close to the entrance of the catacombs, taken by a German officer in 1916. Marcus Massing

by a small triangular shaped wood (which the British later called Wedge Wood) and a farm, know locally as Faffémont Farm and miss-spelt by the British as Falfemont. As this was the name by which it was known to every British soldier who fought at Combles, it will be the spelling hereafter used in the book.

Because of its safe position, Combles was used extensively for billeting troops by the German army. Prior to the Battle of the Somme, German divisions in the line at Montauban and Hardecourt saw Combles as a staging post on their way to the front, using the many cellars and large houses as places for their men to rest. Again, largely because of its position in a hollow, photographic

A shot of shell damage from inside Combles church.

Combles in the early stages of the British bombardment

evidence indicates that the village suffered very little damage until
August 1916, by which time fighting had reached Guillemont only a
few miles away, bringing Combles into direct fire from field guns for
the first time.

Ernst Jünger wrote one of the few German soldiers' memoirs of the
Great War to be translated into English - *Storm of Steel*. A remarkable
character, before the Great War Jünger had run away from home and
enlisted in the French Foreign Legion, deserting to join the German
army as a Lieutenant in 1914. During his period on the Somme he
knew Combles well, and describes his first visit to the village in
August 1916.

> *As far as we could see in the darkness, Combles was utterly
> shot to bits. The damage seemed to be recent, judging by the
> amount of timber among the ruins and the contents of the houses
> slung over the road. We climbed over numerous heaps of debris...
> and reached our quarters. They were in a large shot-riddled
> house. Here I established myself with three sections. The other
> two occupied the cellar of a ruin opposite.*[2]

The next morning he was able to get out and explore the village proper.

> *Heavy artillery had turned a peaceful little billeting town into*

Aerial photograph of Combles taken in early September 1916, showing the size and extent of the village. (IWM)

German soldiers entering the cellar system below Combles town hall, summer 1916. IWM Q.45429

> *a scene of desolation in the course of a day or two. Whole houses had been flattened by single direct hits or blown up so that the interiors of the rooms hung over the chaos like the scenes on a stage. A sickly scent of dead bodies rose from many of the ruins, for many civilians had been caught in the bombardment and buried beneath the wreckage of their homes. A little girl lay dead in a pool of blood on the threshold of one of the doorways.*[3]

Unlike the villages close to the British lines, which were evacuated and

Combles war memorial in front of the modern town hall. The original church was just behind, as was the entrance to the catacombs.

the civilians moved out to other locations, the Germans do not appear to have followed a similar practice on the Somme front. Many German memoirs and regimental histories refer to the deaths of French men and women through British shell-fire, and indeed the war memorial in Combles lists several names of local people who died in such circumstances.

Jünger went on to describe a feature of Combles well used by the Germans and which would eventually become well known to both British and French troops.

> The square in front of the ruins of the church had been particularly hard hit. Here was the entrance to the catacombs, a very ancient underground passage with recesses here and there in which were crowded the staffs of all the units engaged. It was said that the civilians had opened up the entrance with pickaxes when the bombardment began. It had been walled up and kept secret from the Germans during the whole of their occupation.[4]

These catacombs were a common feature in many French villages, and such tunnels often dated back many hundreds of years. In most cases the Germans knew about them, and indeed at various stages during the war published a staff guide to them entitled *Unterirdische Anlagen (Katakomben) in Nordfrankreich*[5]. Once known about the ones here at Combles were used, as Jünger states, as a headquarters by German

Names of French civilians from Combles killed during the war.

GUILLEMONT   HENRI
    1920 (SUITES DE LA GUERRE)
STIEVET   DESIRE
MORTS   EN   CAPTIVITE
CAUDRON   EUGENE
DARTUS   LEON
MARCHANDISE   CHARLES
MOLLET   OCTAVE
VILTARD   AUGUSTE
VOYER   EUGENE
FOLLY   FLORENT

divisions in the line at Guillemont-Ginchy. Photographic evidence also shows that a German field hospital, similar to an RAMC Advanced Dressing Station, was also established within them. One of the entrances was below the town hall (Mairie) and another near the church.

As the fighting around Guillemont intensified, Combles came under more regular shell fire. Jünger recalled that from his billet,

> ... the view through the broken windows showed the square utterly deserted, and ploughed up by the shells... The artillery fire that raged round the place without ceasing deepened the gloom of this appalling picture. Now and then the gigantic crashed of a 38-centimetre [British 15-inch] shell dominated the tumult; whereupon a hail of splinters swept through Combles, clattering through the branches of the trees, or striking on the walls of the few houses that were still left standing, and bringing down the slates from the roofs... In the course of the afternoon the firing increased to such a degree that single explosions were no longer audible. There was nothing but one terrific tornado of noise.[6]

Jünger and his comrades, and the many German units sheltering in Combles, thereafter took shelter in the numerous cellars and sections

German map of the catacombs below Combles drawn by the 1st Bavarian Pioneer Regiment in March 1916. (Tom Fairgrieve)

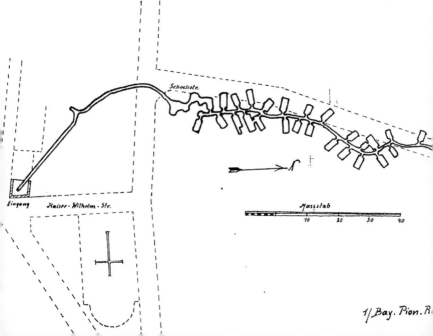

of the catacombs. The bombardment increased to such an extent that to venture outside into one of the streets meant certain death. Hundreds of men were therefore confined to their shelters, and this *trommelfeuer* (drumfire), as the Germans called it, caused at least one man in Jünger's 73rd Hanoverians to go mad.

Following a tour of the line in front of Guillemont, the Hanoverians returned to Combles. It would be Ernest Jünger's last visit. Billeted once more in a cellar, he found the shelling less severe and managed to find a peach tree where he gathered in some fruit for his men. After exploring a few houses, he returned to his billet where his platoon were cooking in a room above their cellar.

> *I had scarcely joined them when there was a loud report in front of the door of the house, and at the same moment I felt a violent blow on my left calf. Shouting out that I was hit, I jumped down the cellar steps with my pipe still in my mouth... There was a ragged hole in my putties, from which blood ran on to the ground. On the other side there was a round swelling of a shrapnel bullet under the skin. The men bound me up and took me under fire to the catacombs, where our surgeon-major-general took me in hand.*[7]

Evacuated by field ambulance, Jünger would not return to his unit until 1917. He survived the war, wrote several books about his experiences, and died in 1997.

The Battle of the Somme

The Battle of the Somme needs no explanation here. Readers of the **Battleground Europe** series and even the casual military enthusiast will be well aware of its causes, and they need not be repeated. How the fighting reached Combles does need some background, however.

The right flank of the British army was one of the few sectors of the Somme battlefield where any success was achieved on the opening day of the 'Big Push' on 1st July 1916. This advance, from the British positions at Maricourt towards Montauban, by the 18th (Eastern) and 30th Divisions, achieved all its objectives and if reserves had been forthcoming in the late afternoon of 1st July, Bernafay Wood to the east could also have been taken. However, no reserves came up and the wood fell three days later. On their right flank were the French troops of the 39th Division, who advanced and took Hardecourt-aux-Bois and Maltz Horn Farm.

Once Bernafay Wood was in British hands by the 3rd July, the next obvious objective to the east was the neighbouring Trones Wood.[8] This

Personnel from a German artillery unit take shelter in Combles Quarry, 1916. (Tom Gudmestad)

proved much tougher to crack, and despite several attempts the wood did not fall until it was cleared by the 18th (Eastern) Division on 14th July. From here successive attacks were launched on Guillemont, and losses on both sides mounted. Ernst Jünger recalled the battlefield in late August 1916 from the German soldier's perspective.

British RFA supply column on a road in Guillemont, September 1916.

The ground all road, as far as the eye could see, was ploughed by shells. You could search in vain for one wretched blade of grass. This churned up battlefield was ghastly. Among the living lay the dead. As we dug ourselves in we found them in layers stacked one upon the top of another. One company after another had been shoved into the drum-fire and steadily annihilated. The corpses were covered with the masses of soil turned up by the shells, and the next company advanced in the place of the fallen.[9]

Guillemont finally fell to elements of the 20th (Light), and attached battalions of the 16th (Irish) Divisions on September 3rd 1916. Attacking from the old positions west of the village, units of 59th Brigade followed the British barrage closely and were able to reach the forward trenches quickly, surprising the Germans. Fighting for the village itself was swift and decisive, some battalions reaching their objectives within as little as twenty minutes. Mopped-up by the 10th Bn King's Royal Rifle Corps, battalions pushed on and dug-in beyond the cemetery along the Ginchy - Maurepas road. For the first time British troops had a clear view to Bouleaux and Leuze Woods – and beyond that was Combles.

Memorial to the 20th (Light) Division, Guillemont.

Falfemont Farm

On the right flank of this attack was the 5th Division. This formation was a regular army division, and had been in France since August 1914, being the veteran of numerous engagements. It had undergone many changes by the time of the Somme and had some of its regular battalions exchanged for New Army units. Most recently it had taken part in some very costly operations at High Wood, and many units were still under strength. In the fighting east of Guillemont, the objective given to the division's commander, Major General

Operations map of the 5th Division at Falfemont Farm, September 1916.

R.B.Stephens, was to take the German second line of trenches to include Falfemont Farm and Wedge Wood. If circumstances permitted, his troops were also to advance on the south-west corner of Leuze Wood and effect an entry. Here they might also be able to link up with French troops on their right, who were to advance on a position known as Savernake Wood. The units selected for the attack were elements of 15th and 95th Brigades. They moved into the line east of Guillemont on the evening of 2nd/3rd September, in preparation for the attack taking place on the morning of the 3rd. The whole attack was part of the next stage of the Battle of the Somme, and in this area a joint operation with the French Army.

Zero Hour was set for 9am on the 3th September, and at this time the 2nd KOSB advanced directly on Falfemont Farm. The French unit on the right had not advanced, and as the KOSBs moved towards the visible ruins of the farm, they came under terrific fire from the machine-gun sections of 164th Infantry Regiment (IR) who defended it. In addition enfilade fire from Savernake Wood stopped the men when they were 100 to 150 yards from their objective. Meanwhile a heavy German barrage from Combles was laid down on the British forward positions at Angle Wood, then occupied by 15th Royal Warwicks (2nd Birmingham Pals) who were in immediate reserve. Following the failure of the KOSBs to reach the farm, the Pals were then called up to provide support. 1st Cheshires, who were at the ready in Chimpanzee Valley, then moved up to the firestorm surrounding Angle Wood as the Warwicks moved off.

The next attack went in at noon, with the 1st DCLI and 12th Gloucesters (Bristol City Battalion) of 95th Brigade on the left, and 14th and 15th Royal Warwicks on the right near Falfemont Farm. The 95th Brigade advance was successful, but the two Warwicks battalions again came under terrific machine-gun and shell fire around the farm itself. However, 14th Bn managed to reach some old German gun pits, here taking seventeen prisoners and two '08 Maxim guns. They also managed to gain a foothold in a circular German trench just south of Wedge Wood and immediately north-west of Falfemont Farm, which was only a few hundred yards away.

95th Brigade had meanwhile made a footing in the sunken lane that ran north from, and was just in front of, the shattered stumps of Wedge Wood following a superb suppressive barrage which inflicted heavy casualties upon the defenders of this position. More than 150 prisoners were taken, and passed back through Guillemont. Following this success it was decided to continue with the advance, and push on to the farm. But given that the elements of both brigades now occupied a fairly small area and were in some places mixed up, it was impossible to organise this and issue orders until 6.30pm, by which time semi-darkness had descended on the battlefield. This attack was led by the 1st Cheshires on the right and 1st Bedfords on the left. Wedge Wood was finally cleared, but the Cheshires were once more held up by the machine-gun fire in the direction of the farm. Following more than an hour's fighting, by which time it was totally dark, the operation was halted and the units concerned passed orders to dig in and consolidate the existing positions gained.

Fresh Operation Orders were passed down ordering a second main attack to take place at 3.10pm on the 4th September, the next day. 95th Brigade was to advance on German trenches that ran beyond Wedge Wood to near the farm, and 15th Brigade was to push through and again try and reach the previous objective at the south-west corner of Leuze Wood. Two battalions from the 16th (Irish) Division were attached for these operations[10]. Following some last minute changes, the men finally went over the top at 6.30pm. Such attacks in darkened conditions, which helped to screen the advance, were now becoming more common by this period of the Somme fighting. The lead battalions of 95th Brigade were 1st East Surreys, supported by two companies of 1st Devons. They reached their objective, Valley Trench, without difficulty. Indeed, the Surrey's commanding officer recorded that the only casualties were from "... our own shrapnel."[11] The Devons moved on, and by 7.30pm had reached the edge of Leuze Wood, just south of the Guillemont-Combles road. Intense British shelling of the position, the artillery not knowing that British troops had advanced that far, prevented access to the wood itself. By this stage in the war attacking battalions were normally allocated a FOO (Forward Observation Office) from one of the division's artillery units to act as a liaison officer between the infantry and the gunners, enabling the latter to assist on a more flexible basis. The FOO attached to the Devons signalled back to his field battery to cease firing, and the infantry moved in among the shattered trees effecting the first entry into Leuze Wood. Few Germans were encountered, although German sources show that the second and third battalions of the 73rd Hanoverians were in the vicinity. They may well have been checked by the same barrage which had initially stopped the Devons.

However, there were always casualties. Amongst those wounded was Corporal Edwin Dwyer VC. A regular soldier, Dwyer had gained his Victoria Cross at Hill 60, near Ypres, in April 1915. He had been badly wounded, and spent much of the following year at recruiting marches while he recovered. Finally he was passed fit to rejoin his old battalion in the summer of 1916. Just before he departed for the front once more he was persuaded to make a voice recording, very rare for a young working class lad in those days. In this recording he described the fighting in 1914, the retreat from Mons and ends up singing a popular soldier's song of the day, 'We're Here Because We're Here'. This recording is all the more poignant as Dwyer died of his wounds received near Falfemont Farm, and this is perhaps the only known voice recording of an other ranks soldier who fell in the Great War.[12]

In the 15th Brigade, 1st Bedfords and 1st Cheshires had succeeded in entering German trenches north of the farm. 1st Norfolks on their right had encountered the continuing problem with the machine-guns that defended this position, and had been held up largely by fire from the direction of Combles ravine. They later reported,

> *A & B Coys assaulted. Very heavy machine gun fire opened on them immediately. Capt Francis and a few men succeeded in reaching the SW corner of the Farm but were bombed out – and the remainder of the attack was held up by cross machine gun fire. The situation now became very involved, as all the officers but two were either killed or wounded, and the advance over a 600 yard front was very split up as the only way to go on was by crawling from shell hole to shell hole.[13]*

While the Norfolks were pinned down, the Bedfords bombed their way via various German trenches into the northern and western part of the rubble that once had been Falfemont Farm. In doing so they took 130 prisoners of 164th IR, and more importantly several of the machine-guns that had held up the advance. 16th Royal Warwicks (3rd Birmingham Pals) were then brought up, and during the night they dug saps out towards the farm in preparation for the final advance on the position. The men of the Norfolks had been warned to dig in, some of them only 50 yards from the Germans, and rush the farm when the next attack went in. But there were problems with the battlefield following all this concentrated fighting.

> *The ground between our trenches and the objective was a mass of shell holes, and very bad going at the best of times – but heavy rain set in during the night (which was also an exceptionally dark one) and added to this the men had become completely exhausted.[14]*

During the night, assisted by the Warwicks, the men from A Company of 1st Norfolks finally effected an entry into the farm. By 3am the next

An isolated field grave on the battlefield close to Leuze Wood, September 1916. (IWM Q.4316)

morning (5th September) the farm was finally in British hands. The commanding officer of the battalion wisely sent forward stores of grenades and ammunition for the Lewis machine guns, five of them now chiefly defended the newly won ground. By 7.30am the whole position was occupied; and the French troops on the right had at last come up and joined the Norfolks. Attempts to move the machine gun sections forward to a nearby small quarry north-east of the farm towards Leuze Wood were met with disaster when the officer leading the party was killed, and one gun knocked out.[15] A further Lewis gun was hit by shell fire reducing the available fire-power, but no German counter-attacks were forthcoming. That night the battalion was relieved, but given the tactical situation on the ground, two officers and a hundred men were left behind until the next day. The remainder went into some old trenches near Hardecourt. Casualties for the 1st Norfolks were heavy, with six officers killed and seven wounded, along with 356 Other Ranks killed, wounded and missing. *Soldiers Died* shows that 108 of these latter casualties were killed or died of wounds – a high figure which reflects the close nature of the final combat in and around Falfemont Farm.[16]

The Push Towards Leuze Wood

Following the entry of 95th Brigade into the western edge of Leuze Wood, the attacks were now directed up the valley running towards the southern edge of the wood and outskirts of Combles. On 5th September 1st Devons were actively digging-in in the wood, and two and a half companies of the Somerset Light Infantry on loan from 20th (Light) Division were brought up to plug the gap between 95th and 15th Brigades. On the right 16th Royal Warwicks had pushed out patrols beyond the farm. A report came back to Brigadier General M.N.Turner that,

> ... the Germans have retired altogether, and the 18-pdr barrage prevents us going forward, please have it stopped at once. A new Brigade or Division should now go right through us; there is no German anywhere to be seen, and I think they must have retired completely.[17]

At the same time another report on the 95th Brigade front from the commander of 1st Bedfords came back. He informed brigade that,

> ... I am convinced that fresh troops taking over the line today could push on some miles. The Boche is disorganised. A prisoner told me that many of their field guns had been taken away.[18]

At once a message was passed down to XIV Corps headquarters advising them of these reports and requesting fresh troops to come up. Meanwhile the only local reserve were the battalions of the Royal Irish Fusiliers on loan from 16th (Irish) Division. The 7th Bn assisted 1st Devons in taking some trenches in the south-west corner of the wood and the 8th sent forward strong patrols. They were too few in number to effect any kind of breakthrough as had been suggested.

But the call for fresh troops had not gone unnoticed at XIV Corps. Fresh troops were required, and fresh troops were found. Resting close to this sector of the Somme battlefield were the territorial battalions of the 56th (London) Division. As early as the night of 5th September elements of the Kensingtons and London Scottish made their way into Leuze Wood. Fresh troops for a breakthrough. The London boys had arrived.

---

1 For further information on the background to the London Regiment see: Reed, Paul 'Londons Saturday Night Soldiers' in Stand To! Number 19.

2 Jünger, E. The Storm of Steel (Pelham Library 1941) p.93.

3 Jünger op cit. p.94.

4 ibid.

5 Anon. Unterirdische Anlagen (Katakomben) in Nordfrankreich (Herausgegeben im

Auftrag des A.O.K.2. Februar 1918). Among other locations, an example of this fascinating book is in the library of the Imperial War Museum, London.

6 Jünger op cit. p.95.

7 Jünger op cit. p.105-106.

8 For further details of this action see Stedman, M. <u>Battleground Europe:</u> Guillemont (Pen & Sword 1998)

9 Jünger op cit. p.99.

10 The 7th Royal Irish Fusiliers were attached to 15th Brigade, and 8th Royal Irish Fusiliers to the 95th.

11 Quoted in Miles, W. <u>Military Operations France and Belgium 1916</u> Vol 2 (Macmillan and Co 1938) p.258.

12 Cpl Edward Dwyer died of wounds in an Advanced Dressing Station and is buried at Flat Iron Copse Cemetery, close to Mametz Wood and some distance from where he was wounded. It is possible his grave was moved there in the 1920s. The recording he made was once available on a record called, <u>Songs and Voices of the Great War</u> which appears to have been deleted.

13 <u>War Diary</u> 1st Bn Norfolk Regiment, PRO WO95/1573.

14 ibid.

15 The officer was 2/Lt T. Brown who was killed in action. He is buried in Delville Wood Cemetery, Longueval.

16 <u>Soldiers Died in the Great War 1914-19</u> CD ROM (Naval & Military Press 1998).

17 'Report On Operations Carried Out By 5th Division from 3rd to 5th September 1916' page 5, PRO WO95/1513.

18 ibid. p.5.

Chapter Two

FIRST ASSAULT ON LEUZE WOOD

The Arrival of 56th (London) Division

The 56th (London) Division were not new to the Somme. Following their formation in the Spring of 1916, they had moved down to the northernmost sector of the Somme battlefield opposite Gommecourt. It was here that they made their fateful attack on 1st July 1916, a day in which the Division suffered more than 4,700 casualties.[1] Reinforcement drafts followed, made up of men from second line London Regiment battalions, often from units not serving in the 56th Division. For example, a couple of weeks after 1st July the 9th Londons (QVR) received a draft of men from the 8th (Post Office Rifles), a battalion which was actually part of the 47th (2nd London) Division. Several of the men from this draft were killed during the week following their arrival in a bombardment of the British front line. None of them had had time to remove their PO Rifles cap badges or shoulder titles, and in army records they were still recorded as 8th Londons. After the war their names appeared in *Soldiers Died* as 8th Londons, their medals were engraved 8th Londons and their headstones also retain their original regiment's cap badge! Some of the

General map of 56th (London) Division operations at Combles, September 1916.

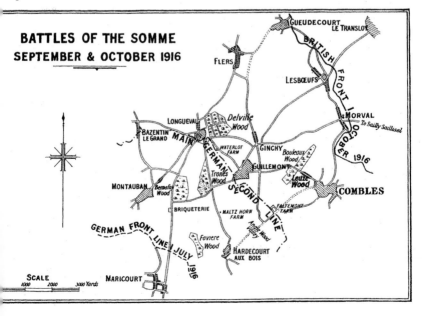

old hands in the battalions of 56th Division resented the arrival of these men from, effectively, other regiments, especially when it was learnt that many of the drafts allocated for the division had been sent elsewhere. However, these 'new' men soon merged into the ranks of their adopted unit, and gave a good account of themselves at Combles. The feared loss of morale and unit cohesion by mixing one regiment with another was not apparent at this stage.

The division left the Gommecourt sector on 20th August 1916, relieved by the 17th (Northern) Division, and moved back to rest billets near Doullens. From here it moved to St Riquier and came under the command of X Corps for a period of rest, refitting and training. St Riquier was close to the town of Abbeville, on the river Somme itself, and miles from the front. This area had not been touched by the hand of war, and aside from the fact that the only men to be seen were either young boys or old men (the rest serving in the French Army), life appeared normal to the men of the London Division as they marched into the area.

Once here duties were fairly simple, but rest rarely meant true rest in the British Army, as the historian of the division later noted,

> *... there were, it is true, no trenches to man, no sentry groups by day and night, but there was always work to be done.*[2]

The division was spread out in a number of small villages in the St Riquier area, but the tempting prize of the town of Abbeville was only a few miles away. Many men hoped there would be an opportunity to explore the well known benefits of any French town, but Aubrey Smith of the London Rifle Brigade noted that upon arrival in their billeting village, Canchy, instructions were issued at once that Abbeville was out of bounds, except for army business. He recalled,

> *... not only that, but we were not allowed even to leave Canchy without obtaining a pass, a rather needless regulation as Abbeville was the only place outside our area to which anyone had the slightest desire to go.*[3]

But there was another reason behind this restriction in movement, which the men of the London division were about to discover.

Training With Tanks

In an era where Heath-Robinson's fantastic cartoons depicted all sorts of weird and wonderful machines of the future, the concept of an armoured fighting vehicle of any description might have seemed to the average soldier part of this very culture of fantasy. But the idea of some type of armoured vehicle had been in the planning stage for some time,

Mark I female tank (twin machine guns) in battlefield camouflage and with anti-grenade nets on the roof. It was with this type of vehicle that the London division trained at St Riquier.

and armoured cars already existed on the outbreak of the war, several of them being despatched to join the British Expeditionary Force in 1914. Wheeled vehicles proved useless in the conditions of trench warfare, with vast crater zones of shell holes, but it was clear that some type of weapon of this nature was needed. Tracked agricultural vehicles were developed and eventually a Mark I 'Land Ship' was ready for production by 1916. It eventually took the name 'tank', as in order to keep the result of the product secret, the Land Ship was initially referred to as a 'water tank' upon arrival in France. Despite many accounts to the contrary, Douglas Haig commanding the BEF in France, and many of his senior officers, were actually very keen and supportive towards this project. By late August 1916 it was obvious to Haig that the Somme battlefield would be a useful proving ground for the new weapon, and that the current sluggish nature of the offensive needed an injection of something to kick start it again, and the tank might just prove to be the solution. A substantial order for tanks was therefore placed with the manufacturers in Lincoln, and they began to arrive in France by late August 1916.

One of the first formations to encounter the tank was the 56th (London) Division. While it was on rest around St Riquier the division was selected to be one of the first to be trained alongside the new weapon. The first the London Rifle Brigade knew about it was when they were assembled on parade.

No 3 Platoon, A Company, 1/5th Londons (London Rifle Brigade) during training at Blendecques. Soon these men would be thrown into the maelstrom of Leuze Wood.

> *The C.O. addressed us and said that we were about to see a very wonderful thing that day and that no reference was to be made to it in any letters, as it was a secret, a statement which roused considerable curiosity... What I saw from a hillock that day was a number of black dots giving forth smoke or steam, crawling across the plain where the infantry were practising.*[4]

Aubrey Smith was far from the only observer that day. Not only had Haig himself appeared to watch, but the French commander Joffre and the Prince of Wales as well. What they saw was the 1/7th Middlesex co-operating in a training exercise with the tanks, in which they practised advancing on a German position. A battlefield was laid out using white tape to represent trenches and the men were given orders,

> *... that the tanks would cross our front line at zero hour, and would be followed by the first infantry wave one minute later. The second wave would start at zero plus three minutes; the third wave at zero plus five minutes; the fourth wave at zero plus six minutes. The infantry were instructed to advance in short rushes up to, but not beyond, the tanks - unless a tank broke down, when they were to proceed as if it was not there.*[5]

Having only been in France for less than a week, the crews of these vehicles were still getting used to them, and although considered a success, the training was often hampered by mechanical failure and breakdown. But yet amongst the common rank and file, these were already seen as war winning weapons, and wild rumours predicted that the tanks could,

> ... *run across any trench and tear up barbed wire like paper...*
> *They'll run straight into any house and crush it flat... And trees*
> *less than sixteen inches in diameter will bend like matchwood*
> *when they run against it.*[6]

Experience would prove otherwise, both for the London territorials and the tank crews of the Heavy Branch Machine Gun Corps (as they were then known). For now it gave the men some hope that the war was going in their favour, and that casualties on the battlefield might be reduced by such a weapon.

As the course of training continued every battalion in the division practised with the tanks. Another new weapon which had appeared on the Western Front in 1915, the flame-thrower, was by now common place on the battlefield. As the division was now made up of a large number of post-Gommecourt reinforcements who had never even heard of, or seen the weapon in action, examples were brought up and a training course built around these fearsome devices as well. Finally the famous Colonel R.B.Campbell, in later years caricatured by the war poet Siegfried Sassoon, came to lecture the battalions. He was the acknowledged expert in the army on bayonet fighting and spoke to the men,

> ... *in his own wonderful way, inspiring every man with the*
> *thrilling hopes of the use that he might be able to make of the*
> *weapon.*[7]

The old soldiers who had been out since 1914 knew that, up the line, the major use for the bayonet was opening tins of jam and as a peg to hang your equipment on in a dug out.

Up The Line

Despite the experience with the tanks, when orders came for the division to return to the Somme front in early September, it was to be without the Heavy Branch MGC. Their own training was yet to be completed, as the tanks were considered not quite ready to be committed to battle. Instead the Londoners left the St Riquier area, and moved via Bray to Citadel Camp and Happy Valley just outside Albert. The whole area was a hive of activity, as the Division's historian later noted.

> *No one will ever be able to describe in adequate fashion the*

scene behind the Somme battle front. Piccadilly in the height of the season, with its slow moving and ever-stopping traffic, may give some idea of the state of the roads - only one must substitute army carts, limbers, lorries... and one must substitute a loose stone road covered with six inches of mud, and holes three feet deep filled with water... The infantry threaded its way in single file through this mass of dirty carts, and sweating men and horses, and overheated motor lorries, halting sometimes for hours... The whole country seemed pulsing with life and effort.[8]

Here they moved into the Nissen huts of Citadel Camp until orders arrived for the Division to relieve the 5th Division in the line between Leuze Wood and Falfemont Farm. These orders were issued as a direct result of reports coming back from the front line to XIV Corps headquarters (see chapter one), reports which stated that the Germans were few in number out in front, and that a general retirement may be in progress.

Two battalions were selected to move up into this sector immediately on the night of the 6th September, the Kensingtons and the London Scottish. The Kensingtons were moving up to take over Falfemont Farm. Jack Tucker was serving with the battalion at this time and later recalled the journey up.

We were now very near our destination. Dawn found us at the end of a valley. Turning left we entered another long narrow valley with steep sides to both flanks. This was named Angle Wood Valley, known to us as 'Death Valley'. The top of the ridge on our left had shallow dug-outs and strong points overlooking the huge plain over which we had travelled. On the right was a steep embankment facing the enemy lines, and half way along the ridge of the valley was a small shattered wood or copse called Wedge Wood. The far end of the valley rose to Leuze Wood, or as we called it, 'Lousy Wood'.[9]

As they moved into the shallow trenches that surrounded the rubble of the farm, they relieved the Royal Irish Fusiliers attached to 5th Division. Tucker noticed that the whole battlefield was covered in the bodies of soldiers of both sides killed in the recent fighting.

The ground just over the ridge of Death Valley was scattered with the Irish dead, mainly young fellows who mostly appeared to have been killed by concussion, tiny streaks of blood having issued from their ears and noses. Others had been killed by machine gun and shrapnel fire... One middle aged Irishman was sitting upright in a shell hole, one side of his head shining pink, where half his scalp had been torn off... [at] Wedge Wood... this trench was full of German dead, Prussian Guards. For some peculiar reason they were minus their tunics, wearing new white vests. The bodies were lying several deep, and we had to walk over them in order to proceed along the trench.[10]

It was a grim introduction to the realities of the battlefield for the young reinforcements within the battalion.

The London Scottish had moved up into Leuze Wood itself,

Aerial intelligence photograph showing the ground around Bouleaux and Leuze Woods during the period of the first attacks in early September 1916. (WM) relieving the other battalion of the Royal Irish Fusiliers. Reserve companies were left at Wedge Wood while the leading companies moved into the wood. At the moment of relief the Germans launched a bombing attack which threatened to evict all of them from the wood, but the Irishmen beat it back despite heavy losses, and were able to hand over the trenches to the London Scottish. However, these were trenches largely in name only, most of them being a series of two foot scrape holes dug in the haste of operations by units of the 5th Division when they first entered the wood. Thus among the first duties upon arrival was to make these positions more permanent. The battalion's front now extended from a trench north of the Combles road on the edge of Bouleaux Wood, into the main body of Leuze Wood itself. Next morning the French launched an operation to capture Combles, which failed. In support, British artillery laid a barrage on the village and many of the shells fell short onto Leuze Wood and the trenches held by the London Scottish. Captain A.H.Macgregor attempted to stop the gunners by sending back messages, but this failed and the shelling, and casualties, continued. Meanwhile new trenches were being prepared alongside Bouleaux Wood, and Sergeant Smith of B Company was engaging the enemy ahead with a small party of men giving covering fire to those digging in. Smith himself killed eight Germans, and took a further three prisoner. That night the London Scottish were relieved by the Queen Victoria Rifles (QVR), and moved back to Wedge Wood and then Maltzhorn Farm. This short period just holding the line in the wood had cost the battalion nearly a hundred casualties, of which some thirty were killed in action or died of wounds.[11]

The QVRs, commanded by Lieutenant Colonel V.W.F.Dickins DSO VD, occupied Leuze Wood on the night of 7th September. The relief had been a difficult one, and Dickins and his men had wandered around in the dark for some time before they could find any landmarks to orientate themselves. Drizzling rain set in once the positions were occupied, but next day was thankfully a quiet one.

The First Attack - 9th September 1916
The next phase of the Somme advance was to begin on the afternoon of 9th September. XIV Corps headquarters had planned a two division assault, with 16th (Irish) Division on the left who were to move forward and take the village of Ginchy. Previously this Division had been split up and allocated to several formations, but finally - and much depleted through battle losses - it was placed again under the

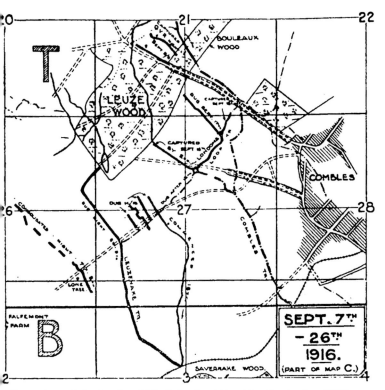

Operations of the London Rifle Brigade at Combles, September 1916.

command of Major General Hickie and operated as an independent formation. On the right were the 56th (London) Division who were to attack from Leuze Wood, and up the Combles valley. Zero hour was set for 4.45pm, as many of the assaulting units were still coming up and getting in to position, and a heavy bombardment was placed on key positions in the German line opposite the two divisions.

In the London division itself there were worries that an attack across the ground as it stood might lose direction, as the whole front was very obscure with many gaps and zigzagging lines of trenches - some of which actually joined up with German ones. However, there was no way round this and the operation was carried out regardless. Orders passed down to the brigades dictated that 168th Brigade on the left, who were in a line on the Guillemont-Combles road, were to make a right form movement, pushing towards the Ginchy road (in fact a track leading from one corner of Leuze Wood to the village of Ginchy). On the right 169th Brigade were to advance towards Combles, and capture a system of trenches close to the south-east corner of the wood and near a sunken lane, and then advance their line a short way through Bouleaux Wood if possible.

The leading battalion in the attack was the London Rifle Brigade (LRB). Commanded by the newly promoted Acting Lieutenant Colonel R.H.Husey, it had moved up on 7th September and relieved the Kensingtons near Falfemont Farm. On the evening of the next day, they assisted the QVRs in Leuze Wood itself, making a bombing attack to clear the south-east sector. However, this was thrown back later. Orders arrived to continue with the advance next day on the 9th, and the battalion found itself with,

> ... *Leuze Wood on the left of the LRB position, and was connected with Combles on the right by a sunken road, on the British side of which was German wire, and on the further side the enemy's trench. The road was occupied, and anyone approaching the wire was heavily bombed at once.*[12]

The original orders received were to attack head on from the LRB front line to the sunken road and the German trench, and push on to take another German position known as The Loop. However, towards Zero Hour, these orders were changed, now ordering a move north into the wood and to attack the sunken lane and the trench from the flank. Duly at 4.45pm the advanced companies moved into the wood, with B Company on the right and C on the left, with A in support. As they crossed the open ground towards the wood they came under terrific machine-gun fire and a well directed artillery barrage. Entering the wood the attack went on and reached the German trench, but by this time the losses were heavy, particularly among the officers, and nearly 400 all ranks had been killed or wounded.

One of the officers wounded in this action was Captain Gilbert Nobbs. Nobbs was commanding a company, and had only been at the front for a matter of a few weeks, and had joined the battalion during its training session at St Riquier. Previously he had served with the 2/5th Londons in England, but had been with the LRB since 1914. Prior to that he had some service in the ranks, had resigned and gone to Canada, where he had been commissioned as an officer. Back in England when the war broke out, Nobbs was immediately promoted to the rank of Captain. But so far active service had eluded him, and this was his first time in battle - and was to prove his last. Seriously wounded in the head and blinded, he was taken prisoner by the Germans in the trench at the sunken road. He was eventually repatriated in 1917, and on his return wrote a classic account of his

Leuze Wood after the bombardment. The difficult nature of fighting in this sort of terrain is evident. (IWM Q.49274)

short war entitled *Englishman, Kamerad!* This Great War classic is rarely known, and was last published in the 1930s when extracts were used in *The Great War: I Was There*. An edited account of Nobbs' part in the action for Leuze Wood is reproduced here. It begins after the LRB have moved through Leuze Wood, and were about to cross the ground towards The Loop and the sunken lane.

At last the thunder of our guns towards the German lines confirmed the hour. Zero Hour had arrived; the barrage had begun.

'No 6 platoon will advance.'

The front line jumped up and walked into the open. Wonderful! Steady as a rock, the line was perfect! On the left the front line of C Company had also emerged from the wood; the bombers of No 6 platoon disappeared along the mystery trench. The tut-ut-ut-ut of machine-guns developed from several parts of the square, while the crack of rifles increased in intensity. No 7 platoon jumped up and advanced into the open, followed by the third wave. I extended my runners and followed. What happened next beggars description... hell was let loose on these men.

Barely had I emerged from the wood with my ten runners when a perfect hurricane of shells was hurled at us, machine-guns from several points spraying their deadly fire backwards and forwards, dropping men like corn before the reaper. From all three sides of the square a hurricane of fire was poured into the centre of the square upon us, as we emerged from the wood.

In far less time than it takes to record it, the attacking waves became a mere sprinkling of men. They went on for a yard or two, and then all seemed to vanish; and even my runners, whom I had extended into line, were dropping fast. The situation was critical, desperate. Fearful lest the attack should fail, I ran forward, and collecting men here and there from shell-holes where some had taken refuge, I formed them into a fresh firing line, and once more we pressed forward.

Again and again the line was thinned; and again the survivors, undaunted and unbeaten, re-formed and pressed forward. Men laughed, men cried, in the desperation of the moment. We were grappling with death; we were dodging it, cheating it; we were mad, blindly hysterical. What did anything matter? Farther and farther into the inferno we must press, at any cost, at any cost; leaping, jumping, rushing, we went from shell-hole to shell-hole; and still the fire continued with unrelenting fury.

I jumped into a shell-hole and found myself within ten yards of my objective. My three remaining runners jumped in alongside of me. They were Arnold, Dobson, and Wilkinson. Arnold was done for! He looked up at me with eyes staring and face blanched, and panted out that he could go no further, and I realised that I could count on him no more.

I glanced to the left, just in time to see three Germans not five yards away, and one after the other jump from a shell-hole which formed a short bay to their trench, and run away. Wishing to save the ammunition in my revolver for the hand-to-hand scuffle which seemed imminent, I seized the rifle of Arnold and fired. I missed all three; my hands were shaky.

What was I to do next? The company on my left had disappeared; the trench just in front of me was occupied by the Boche. I had with me three runners, one of whom was helpless, and in the next shell-hole was about six men, who appeared to be the sole survivors of my company. Where were the supports: anxiously I glanced back towards the wood; why did they not come? Poor fellows, I did not know it at the time, but the hand of death had dealt with them even more heavily in the wood than it had with us.

My position was desperate. I could not retire. My orders were

imperative. 'You must reach your objective at any cost.' I must get
there somehow. But even if we got there, how long could I hope
to hold out with such a handful of men? Immediate support I
must have; I must take risks. I turned to brave Dobson and
Wilkinson.

'Message to the supports: Send me two platoons quickly,
position critical.'

Without a moments hesitation they jumped up and darted off
with the message which might save the day. Dobson fell before
he had gone two yards; three paces further on I saw Wilkinson,
the pet of the company, turn suddenly round and fall on the
ground, clutching at his breast. All hope for the supports were
gone.

At this moment the bombing section, which by this time had
cleared the mystery trench, arrived on the right of the objective;
and to my delirious joy I noticed the Germans in the trench in
front of me running away along the trench. It was now or never!
We must charge over that strip of land and finish them with the
bayonet. A moment's hesitation and the tables might again be
turned and all would be lost. The trench in front must be taken by
assault; it must be done. There were six or seven of us left, and
we must do it.

I yelled to the men:

'Get ready to charge, they are running. Come on! Come on!'

I jumped out of the shell-hole, and they followed me. Once
again I was mad. I saw nothing, I heard nothing. I wanted to kill,
kill!

Pf-ung!

Oh my God! I'm hit! I'm blind![13]

Nobbs had been struck by a bullet on his left temple, which had passed
through his head and exited via his right eye. He was completely blind,
and although shouting out to his men he soon realised his position was
hopeless. His badly wounded runner, Arnold, came to his assistance
but he soon drifted into unconsciousness. When he awoke Arnold had
gone, as he had returned towards the British lines only to be taken
prisoner. In a vain attempt to get his captors to assist, a German
stretcher bearer party went out for Nobbs, but did not find him. It was
some time later a German out on patrol found him sitting in the shell
hole and cried out "Englishman, Kamerad!". Nobbs' war was over.

Meanwhile the QVRs had gone in and taken parts of Bouleaux
Wood. Lieutenant Colonel Dickins had been given an objective to

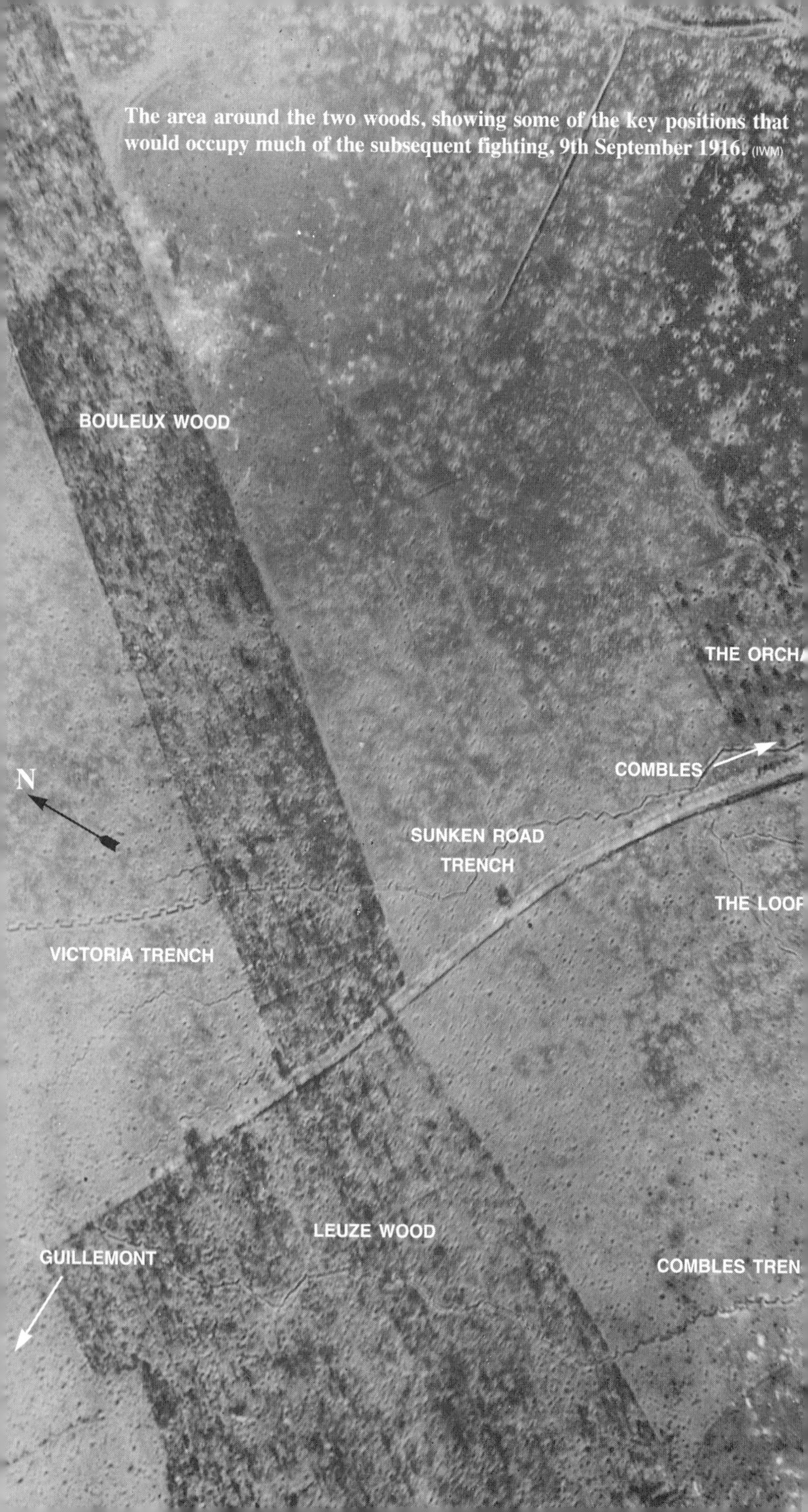

The area around the two woods, showing some of the key positions that would occupy much of the subsequent fighting, 9th September 1916. (IWM)

BOULEUX WOOD

THE ORCH[A]

COMBLES

N

SUNKEN ROAD TRENCH

THE LOOP

VICTORIA TRENCH

LEUZE WOOD

GUILLEMONT

COMBLES TREN[CH]

reach a trench running through the wood, and on to a position 300 yards east of Leuze Wood. This put them on the left of the LRB attack, as described above. In a pre-battle Orders Group in a partially completed mine-shaft behind the forward trenches, a shell rudely interrupted the conference and badly wounded the DADMS (Deputy Assistant Director of Medical Services) of the division, who lost his leg.[14] Despite this the plans were finalised. A and D Companies were to lead the attack, with B in support and C in reserve. A creeping barrage was to be placed in front of the battalion, which it was to follow right to the final objective. An artillery liaison officer was on hand to assist if the barrage plan needed changing, or if the defenders showed stubborn resistance and it needed to be recalled. Before them the ground and wood consisted of,

> ... tall trees, broken and splintered, [which] lay scattered in the undergrowth; a few concrete emplacements lined the western side; vast shell holes reeking of H.E. - and worse things - and here and there limp, shapeless forms covered with blue-bottles and flies, pinned beneath the trees.[15]

In the forward positions as the hour of attack approached, the men of A and D Companies not only had the enemy's artillery to contend with, but the XIV Corps' own heavy artillery. The huge shells from these gun batteries continued to land short of the wood, one bombardment killing 2/Lt R.B. Scott,[16] and blinding 2/Lt W.F. Ogilvie, along with many other ranks. And close to Zero Hour the Germans laid down a heavy bombardment of 5.9-inch and 8-inch shells, inflicting further losses.

At Zero Hour the creeping barrage was laid down in front of the QVRs, and the men moved forward. The Germans returned fire from the wood, and Captains G. Woods and R.F. Davies leading the companies as they went over, were killed almost at once.[17] Captain J.D. Eccles, commanding the support company, also fell mortally wounded.[18] Command now passed to junior officers and Warrant Officers, who led the men forward to the objective.

Back at battalion headquarters, Lieutenant Colonel Dickins awaited news of the attack. He only had to look across to the shell holes that made up the Regimental Aid Post to see that,

> ... the M.O. in shirt sleeves with an old tin hat on the back of his curly head, calmly passed from case to case, hardly appearing to notice the terrific explosions which from time to time snatched one of the casualties from any help that he could give.[19]

At 5pm a message came back to Dickens that the objective appeared to have been reached, despite the casualties. A sergeant-runner then confirmed this, and that the companies were now digging in and consolidating. He also reported that there were no officers left, and Captain Syme was sent forward to take command. He got there to find all the officers killed or wounded and 150 prisoners, who were passed down to Brigade headquarters at Hardecourt.

With Syme in charge, he organised the new position and was confident he could hold it until he saw the Germans amassing for a counter-attack on the right. It was clear to him, despite the fact that he had had no contact with them, that the LRB attack had failed. It also appeared the Germans might be in a position to surround Leuze Wood. A SOS pigeon was despatched to Brigade requesting reinforcements, and Lieutenant Colonel Attenborough of the 1/2nd Londons (Royal Fusiliers) despatched two companies to assist in the area of the LRB operations and effectively 'plug the gap'. At the same time Lieutenant Colonel Shoolbred's Queen's Westminster Rifles (QWR) were also coming up to relieve the survivors of the LRB, and Captain Syme was soon able to report that he no longer feared any German threat on his right.

During that night Syme and his men continued to work on the new position. He immediately christened the new line 'Victoria Trench', which was later changed on trench maps to 'Bully Trench'. Here the QVRs stayed into the morning of 10th September until finally relieved later that day. Casualties in the unit were heavy. Some of the finest and most popular officers had been killed. Captain Davies, killed as he went over, was a veteran of the Boer War and an old boy of Marlborough School. Captain Eccles, killed with him, was only twenty-one, but had previously been wounded in 1915. In the thick of the fight one young officer had distinguished himself, only to be killed. The events leading up to the death of 2/Lt N.Y. Sim were related by Rifleman Surtees of the QVRs.

For outstanding bravery and devotion to duty, I think the following incident should be featured in any record of the QVR. The regiment were attacking in Leuze Wood... and were ordered to advance through the wood. They were successful in gaining and holding their objective, but while consolidating it, came under very heavy shell fire. L/Cpl Boismaison was in charge of a Lewis gun and occupied a smashed up trench which offered but little cover and a small hope of a good gun position. In the same portion of the trench system was a young officer, 2nd Lieut Sim, who had only joined us a few days previous to 'going up'. After the position had been carried we were facing a slight crest and to reach us the enemy had to come into full view, this affording an excellent target. Seeing no chance of securing a good position for the gun this young officer stood with it on his shoulder whilst L/Cpl Boismaison brought it into action with good results, but it was not long before this gallant officer was shot. Nothing daunted and aware of his danger young Boismaison immediately placed the gun over his own shoulder and called upon No 2 to carry on. He obeyed and continued until the cylinder was pierced by a stray piece of shrapnel and the gun rendered useless.[20]

Boismaison was killed later on,[21] and was one of more than sixty other ranks from the QVRs killed in this action. More than twice this number were wounded.

The 1/4th Londons (Royal Fusiliers) were on the right of 168th Brigade's attack. Commanded by Major H.J.Duncan-Teape, the battalion was pivoting on the north section of Leuze Wood and moving forward under a protective creeping barrage in six waves of infantry. By 5.20pm the first objective had been reached with only a few casualties. However, the unit had lost touch with the Rangers on their

On a shattered Somme battlefield, a wounded comrade is assisted in the crossing of an old trench.

left, and by this time the Fusiliers had started to receive fire from this left flank in the form of machine-guns and snipers. Despite this they pushed on to the next objective, which was reached and consolidated under German shell fire. Major Duncan-Teape then sent forward an advanced patrol which established two patrols overlooking the Morval - LesBoeufs road more than two thousand yards ahead of them. There was still no sight of the Rangers, so the company commander present established another line of posts on the left flank of the battalion as protection in case of German counter-attacks. As darkness descended on the battlefield, the shell fire increased and at one stage many casualties occurred when 'friendly fire' (possibly from the 16th (Irish) Division artillery) fell on new line of the battalion. The advanced posts proved their worth that night, as when the Germans approached they were fired on and withdrew; they was greatly assisted when several Lewis gun teams went forward. Here the battalion remained, somewhat out on a limb with their left flank 'in the air', throughout the 10th September until relieved at midnight by the 1/8th Middlesex.[22] Total casualties are not recorded, but *Soldiers Died* shows that seven officers and 58 other ranks were killed.

The 1/12th Londons (Rangers) attacked on the left. Their objective was to cross the Guillemont-Combles road, and the ground north of it heading towards a position called the Ginchy Telegraph - Bouleaux and Leuze Woods being on their right flank as they did so. A brigade of the 16th (Irish) Division would advance on their immediate left flank, the closest battalion being the 7th Inniskilling Fusiliers. At Zero Hour the leading companies left their assembly trenches north of Wedge Wood, and on reaching the area of the road came under very heavy machine-gun and rifle fire. The majority of this fire was coming from a position away to the north-west known as the Quadrilateral. This was sited south of the Ginchy-LesBoeufs road. D Company was taking most of the fire, and linked up with the 7th Inniskillings. Just on a crest of ground north of the road they took cover and returned fire on the enemy. This enabled them to leap forward to an unoccupied trench close to a virtually obliterated track that once ran from Ginchy towards Leuze Wood. Here they consolidated, realising they were going no further. At nightfall they remained in this trench until the 7th Inniskillings were forced back. The officer commanding D Company then realised that his own position would be untenable, and he ordered a withdrawal back to the original assembly trenches.

C Company on the right came under little fire and made more progress. They reached the road near Leuze Wood at 6am and reached

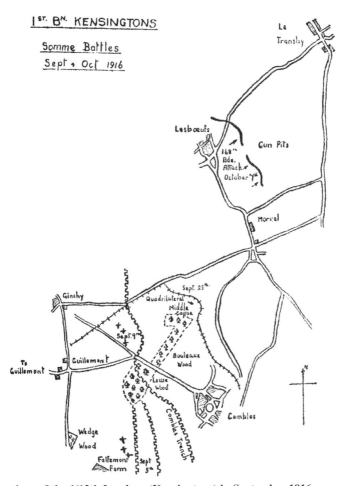

1ST. BN. KENSINGTONS

Somme Battles
Sept + Oct 1916

La Transloy

Lesbœufs

Gun Pits

168th Bde. Attack October 7th

Morval

Ginchy

Sept. 25th.

Quadrilateral

Middle Copse

Sept. 9th

Bouléaux Wood

To Guillemont

Guillemont

Leuze Wood

Combles

N

Wedge Wood

Combles Trench

Falfemont Farm

Sept 5th

Operations of the 1/13th Londons (Kensingtons) in September 1916.

their final objective by a series of planned rushes. However, fire was reaching them from the left flank (towards the Quadrilateral), and this made progress slow and difficult. The objective was reached forty-five minutes later, where a mixed bag of 1/4th Londons, Kensingtons (who were in support - see below) and QVRs were found. This position was consolidated with a number of bomb blocks, organised by the bombers from the battalion and 1/4th Londons. The London Scottish came up on the night of 9th/10th September, and by the next morning a new line was established from the north-west corner of Leuze Wood away to the left in a north-west direction as far as the remains of the light railway line - a front of about 500 yards. Losses in the Rangers had been severe with four officers and 104 other ranks killed,[23] with several times that number wounded.

The 1/13th Londons (Kensingtons) had been in support for this operation, with the bulk of the battalion being back in the Angle Wood - Wedge Wood area. At Zero Hour A and C companies, who had been occupying the lane from Wedge Wood to the Guillemont-Combles road, moved forward and took over the assembly trenches vacated by the Rangers. At the same time B and D companies occupied the positions just left by A and C. Orders came to move forward, A and C moving out into No Man's Land, stepping into a heavy German bombardment which had just begun. They reached the advanced positions and found them full of the dead and wounded of both sides. The Germans were counter-attacking to the left, around a bomb-block in the trench, but it had proved difficult to stay in touch with the Irish troops on the left flank. Jack Tucker recalled,

> ... [we] had lost touch with an Irish battalion on our left, which was afterwards found not to have reached anywhere near the position it was intended to take, having been held up by a very strong German position known as the Quadrilateral. Major Dickens (a grandson of Charles Dickens) endeavoured to lead a party further to the left to contact the Irish, but was unsuccessful and was killed in the attempt. A year later I was to revisit this place and help erect a wooden cross and rail, which I had painted with an inscription in Old English.[24]

Captain Cedric Charles Dickens was indeed buried on the spot by his men in a field grave close to where he fell. Dickens was a pre-war member of the Kensingtons, and had been wounded in the eye at Aubers Ridge in 1915. After recovering he was posted to the 3/13th Londons, and became Jack Tucker's company commander. Tucker remembered that "... his eye was badly affected with a nervous twitch which he asked us not to take notice of."[25] He returned to the Western Front, but did not go over in the attack on Gommecourt on 1st July.

As Jack Tucker mentions, he returned to the area when his battalion was out on rest at Bapaume in 1917, and together with an officer and some old hands made the grave permanent. He recalls in later correspondence[26] that once the job was complete the officer photographed the grave. After the war, the ground on which the cross stood was purchased by the Dickens family. By the 1950s the War Graves Commission were eager to consolidate isolated graves like those of Dickens, and with the permission of the family made a search for the remains. None were found, and although Major Dickens' name was added to the Thiepval Memorial about this time, the cross remained. The author first saw it in 1985, when it was at the tip of a narrow copse in the fields north of the Guillemont-Combles road. The copse hid the cross, which was in very good condition, but surrounded by live shells which farmers had dumped there. In the mid-1990s on the wishes of the Dickens family a further search was made prior to the copse being levelled, and the cross moved closer to a nearby track. Again nothing was found, but the memorial site was made permanent and rededicated, members of the commune of Ginchy and the Dickens family in attendance. The mystery of Major Dickens therefore continues to this day, but despite some claims Tucker was sure it was the correct site. He recalled,

> ... there were several other graves within a few yards - no names - and all had been visited by rats when we returned to place the cross... it is very unlikely anyone would bother to make an empty grave.[27]

As the light faded on 9th September the men of the Kensingtons dug in alongside the other London battalions. Next day their trench was found to be too full of men, and some withdrew to the assembly trenches. B Company on the right, meanwhile, had advanced into Bouleaux Wood to join the QVRs. Here they bombed their way up a trench, and once cleared consolidated the position and held on. The battalion finally came out of the line two days later on the 11th, when relieved by the 1/7th Middlesex. Casualties by this time had mounted to fifteen officers and 282 men.

In summing up, the historian of the 56th Division felt that this first attack on the woods and Combles had failed because,

> ... the attack on the 9th has always seemed like a wild rush in fast-fading light.. the truth of the whole matter was that the enemy defended Combles with desperation.[28]

And it was a desperation that was to take some time to wear down yet.

1. Dudley Ward, C.H. The 56th Division (John Murray 1921)p.47.
2. ibid. p.49.
3. Smith, A. Four Years On The Western Front (Odhams 1922) p.157.
4. ibid. p.158.
5. Dudley Ward op cit. p.51.
6. Smith op cit. p.158.
7. Anon. The History of the London Rifle Brigade 1859-1919 (Constable 1921) p.158.
8. Dudley Ward op cit. p.52.
9. Tucker, J.F. Johnny Get Your Gun: A Personal Narrative of the Somme, Ypres and Arras (William Kimber 1978) p.66.
10. ibid. p.67.

11. <u>Soldiers Died In The Great War 1914-19</u> CD ROM (Naval and Military Press 1998)

12. Anon. <u>The History of the London Rifle Brigade 1859-1919</u> op cit. p.161.

13. Nobbs, G. <u>Englishman, Kamerad! Right of The British Line</u> (Heinemann 1918) p.97-101.

14. This was Major L.M. Purser DSO, RAMC.

15. Cuthbert Keeson, C.A. <u>The History & Records of Queen Victoria's Rifles 1792-1922</u> (Constable 1923)

16. 2/Lt R.B. Scott, 1/9th Londons (QVR), killed in action 9th September 1916. Buried Delville Wood Cemetery.

17. Captain G. Woods and Capt R.F. Davies, 1/9th Londons (QVR), both killed in action 9th September 1916. Both have no known grave, and are commemorated on the Thiepval Memorial.

18. Captain J.D. Eccles MC, 1/9th Londons (QVR), died of wounds at home 27th September 1916. Buried St Marylebone Cemetery, Middlesex, England.

19. Cuthbert Keeson op cit. p.185. The M.O. was Captain B. Clarke, RAMC, who was awarded the MC.

20. ibid. p.188.

21. Rfn J.W.P. Boismaison, 1/9th Londons (QVR), killed in action 9th September 1916. Commemorated on the Thiepval Memorial.

22. Account compiled from the 1/4th London <u>War Diary</u> PRO WO95/2954.

23. <u>Soldiers Died In The Great War 1914-19</u> CD ROM op cit.

24. Tucker op cit. p.74.

25. Letters from Jack Tucker, 1981-1984, in the possession of Normal Revell and made available to the author.

26. ibid.

27. ibid.

28. Dudley Ward op cit. p.60.

Chapter Three

THE FIGHTING CONTINUES

Attack on Loop Trench - the Queen's Westminster Rifles

The position faced by Major General Hull, commanding 56th (London) Division, on the night of 9th /10th September was not an enviable one. His troops on the left flank, where it joined the 16th (Irish), were in an obscure position south of the Ginchy-Morval road. Others on this flank had gained a foothold in Bouleaux Wood. On the right, Leuze Wood was mostly clear, and there was a virtually continuous outpost line from the wood across the valley between Falfemont Farm and Combles. Hull found himself to be "...surrounded by Germans, and probably only protected by the night".[1] There was no alternative but to press on with the attack.

Trench map of the battlefield surrounding Leuze Wood, showing the key positions of Combles Trench and The Loop.

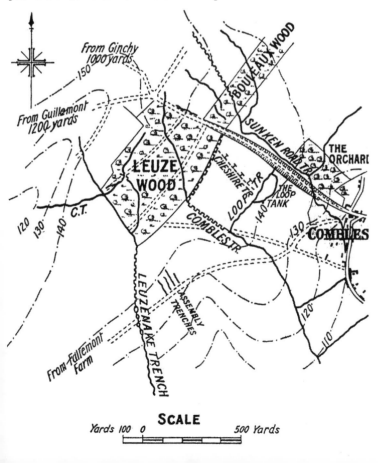

View from Falfemont Farm towards Leuze Wood and The Loop where the QWR fought in September 1916.

The failure of the LRB to take the sunken lane and The Loop meant that another battalion was committed to continue with the task. Brigadier General Coke, commanding 169th Brigade, sent up the Queen's Westminster Rifles (QWR), who arrived around 11pm on the night of September 9th. As they moved into Leuze Wood, orders arrived at battalion headquarters at 1am on the 10th. These orders dictated an advance on a trench on the south-eastern side of the wood, which was Loop Trench. Once in the wood the battalion came under heavy German fire, and there was little time or opportunity in the extreme darkness to reconnoitre the position or the objective. It was known that some maps were inaccurate, so the QWRs commanding officer was worried his men might not actually reach the correct objective.

In the hours approaching Zero Hour, C and D companies of the QWR, who had been selected to make the attack, sent forward advanced parties who returned with valuable information as to the dispositions of the enemy. However, the scouts had not been able to find a communication trench where the majority of the German were meant to be and, despite the approaching light, a thick mist had descended which made further observation impossible. Eventually it was decided to make the attack regardless. Lieutenant Colonel Shoolbred could hardly have been happy with his men going in 'blind'.

Zero Hour was set for 7am, with C and D companies in forward positions towards the eastern edge of Leuze Wood. They both lost men even before the attack began. 2/Lt T.S. Arergis and A.F. Johnston were killed, with 40 other ranks killed or wounded.[2] The companies moved forward; D on the left with its left flank on the sunken road towards Combles, and C on the right. The men moved in wave formation, with platoons in line. The British barrage opened as they jumped off, and while it was successful on the front of D company, it totally failed in the area advanced on by C company. This was largely due to the telephone lines linking the observers with the gun batteries being cut.

Stumbling around in the half light and mist, C company had advanced more than 120 yards from the edge of the wood without seeing any sign of a trench or its objective. However, the German defenders were alerted to a British attack and opened a withering fire on the lines of men from both companies. The artillery barrage had passed them by, and the Germans were able to fire on the QWRs virtually unhindered. Those in the area of The Loop were joined by defenders in a trench alongside the sunken Combles road. After only eighteen minutes into the attack both companies had virtually ceased to exist. A message was received by Lieutenant Colonel Shoolbred that both groups were reduced to a mere twenty-five men and that the situation was hopeless. Shoolbred ordered them back to the cover of the wood, and at 8am wired Brigade headquarters.

> *Situation unchanged. I am lining east side of wood and digging in as far as possible, but it is hard digging in the broken tree stumps. If you will arrange an artillery bombardment on the whole trench that was to be captured, I will then try and bomb round it (i.e. through Combles Trench) afterwards. My companies cannot be collected without great delay and difficulty, and I can see no likelihood of a successful attack as at first attempted. The enemy trench, which was our objective (i.e. Loop Trench) is full of enemy, so a good bombardment should do good; and I hope... to be able to take it by bombing, and then occupy it.[3]*

Brigadier General Coke came up to observe the situation when visibility was better, and the mist had gone. In consultation with Shoolbred, he planned a second advance for 3pm, which would be a bombing attack led by A and B companies of the QWR, and assisted by A Company of Lieutenant Colonel Attenborough's 1/2nd Londons (Royal Fusiliers). They would be supported by the Brigade Trench Mortar Battery and a proper artillery barrage; this latter would lay down a bombardment along the line of the German trench to be attacked. The plan involved the 1/2nd Londons clearing the initial sap

London Scottish marching up to the Somme front.

(Combles Trench) that opened the way to the main objective (Loop Trench) which would be the responsibility of the QWRs.

At 3pm the 1/2nd Londons moved forward and the bombing attack began. A company nearly succeeded in reaching Combles Trench, but in a short space of time lost all its officers.[4] CSM Pellow then took command, but as the artillery barrage seemed to be ineffectual and there was heavy fire coming from the German positions, there was little he could do. Meanwhile the QWRs had followed the Fusiliers, but had also lost most of their bombers from the same heavy fire. The survivors of both units returned to the wood and it was clear the attack had failed. Casualties in the days fighting for the QWR amounted to 307 officers and men. The battalion historian concluded, "... the day had been one of failure".[5]

The London Scottish

While the QWR were advancing on Loop Trench, the London Scottish on the extreme left flank were ordered forward to give some organisation and strength to the join of the 16th and 56th Divisions around the positions held by 1/4th Londons. This area of ground between the south-east corner of Ginchy and Leuze Wood was in a highly confused state. There were no straight lines anywhere, and many of the advance positions were just scattered posts. The exact location of the enemy was not known, and occasionally the Londoners would encounter parties of Irish troops from the neighbouring formation.

The London Scottish had first moved up on the evening of the 9th September, when Captain Syer's D company was attached to the Kensingtons. Syer had gone forward and taken a trench somewhere in the open ground south-east of Ginchy. The order passed to Lieutenant Colonel Lindsay, commanding London Scottish, was to move up to Syer's position and head towards the Quadrilateral. Once there they should go west back towards Ginchy, and in doing so would cut off the remaining Germans in this area. Conditions on the battlefield were difficult, with a very dark night and thick mist and fog, making visibility poor. Furthermore no-one in the battalion had been able to reconnoitre the ground.

In the early hours of the 10th, the battalion moved forward company by company. The lead unit, Captain MacGregor's A company, ran into a German patrol as it approached Syer's trench. A fire-fight over open ground ensued, and although the enemy was beaten off, MacGregor was killed.[6] Furthermore, in the darkness and confusion of battle, the survivors of the company unwittingly did a U-turn and found themselves back at the start positions.

Given the desperate situation, and the inability to make contact easily with friendly forces ahead, Colonel Lindsay sent the battalion scout officer and some of his scouts forward. They found Syer, and got to a position they believed to be the Quadrilateral, where they found a party of Rangers. Some of Syer's men were bombing the Germans on the Rangers left flank, and Syer was able to report that Ginchy had not been entirely cleared by the 16th (Irish) Division. Lindsay realised from this information that he could not carry out his orders as they stood, as with Germans still in and around Ginchy it would be suicidal to try and link up with the Irish units there. As it happened, the fog stayed all day on this part of the battlefield, preventing further observation and movement. It later transpired that the position held by the Rangers was not the Quadrilateral, and that this redoubt was still in German hands. Lindsay's caution had been well founded, but despite this the battalion had still lost two officers killed and more than 100 other rank casualties.[7]

Disaster at Falfemont Farm - 1/2nd Londons

At 6pm the Germans were observed by some of the advance posts to be massing for a counter-attack. B company of 1/2nd Londons was sent forward to act as a mobile reserve, and given instructions to occupy Leuzenake, or 'Q' Trench, running due south from the corner of Leuze Wood. Before moving off, the company commander, Captain Richard Heumann, held an Orders Group in a shell hole near Falfemont Farm, no doubt thinking that lightening would not strike in the same place twice. Nevertheless a shell exploded above the party killing Captain Heumann, his Company Sergeant Major, Bert Mills, and Sergeant Alf Torrence. Three other officers were also wounded, 2/Lt Childs dying shortly afterwards. The only officer left in the company, 2/Lt W.C.Cambray, took command and led the men up to Q Trench.

The wood that now marks the original site of Falfemont Farm.

Captain Richard Heumann had joined the 2nd London Regiment shortly after its formation, in August 1908. Promoted Captain in May 1911, he was part of a detachment from the battalion which had attended the Coronation of George V on 22nd June 1911, Heuman being awarded the Coronation Medal. He went overseas with the battalion in 1915, and had briefly commanded it earlier in 1916. CSM Bertie Mills was born in Hastings, but lived in Lambeth. Like Heumann, he joined the 2nd Londons in 1908 and had been CSM of B Company for some time. Sergeant Alfred William Torrence was living in St Pancras, London, when he joined the 2nd Londons in 1914. Lieutenant David Leslie Childs, the youngest of the four, had been commissioned in February 1915 and served at Gallipoli with the 2/2nd Londons, where he had been their machine-gun officer. When this unit was disbanded in June 1916 he had joined the 1/2nd in time for Gommecourt. Dying of his wounds, Childs was buried in Bronfay Farm Military Cemetery.

At the time the three men (Heumann, Mills and Torrence) were buried in the shell hole where they had been killed and a hasty grave marker placed on the spot. In the years following the Great War there were many such isolated graves, especially in locations like Leuze Wood and Combles, and most were exhumed and moved into larger burial grounds. But on the wishes of the families, these three friends and colleagues remained buried in their wartime grave. The spot was purchased, and a permanent memorial placed on the site. In the years after the Second World War many of these 'private' graves were finally moved into proper cemeteries. However, the War Graves Commission chose not to touch this one and it is there to this day. The experienced company commander, buried with his right hand man CSM Mills, and with a bedrock of the battalion, Platoon Sergeant Torrence: truly a 'comrades grave'. Even today, it is a moving and poignant location.

The Arrival of the 'Die Hards'

The two Middlesex Regiment battalions of the 56th (London) Division had initially been in reserve during the opening phase of the fighting around Combles. Both the 1/7th and 1/8th Battalions were at Billon Farm, bivouacked in the open, while the first assault on Leuze Wood took place. They had then moved up via Maricourt to Casement Trench, near Ginchy, until 10th September, when orders arrived taking the 1/8th nearer to the battle, while the 1/7th took over some old trenches near Wedge Wood.

Following a reconnoitre of the position to be taken over by the

As the battle progressed, little was left of Leuze Wood. (IWM Q.49253)

battalion commander, his Adjutant and all the company commanders (one of whom, Captain A.Tomlinson, being wounded in the process), the 1/8th took over a position in front of Leuze Wood and west of Bouleaux Wood from elements of both the 168th and 169th Brigades. Here they remained, under shell fire from Combles, until the late afternoon of the 11th September, when orders were received to make an attack on a group of trenches close to the Ginchy - Morval road. The plan was to link up with units from the Guards Division, who had passed the Quadrilateral on the left flank and were moving into the gap between LesBoeufs and Morval villages. Captain J.D. White's B Company led the attack, followed by Captain G.W. Tremlett and A Company. C and D were ordered to hold the original front line while the attack was in progress, and support the other companies with their Lewis guns and bombing sections. Both White and Tremlett reached their initial objective but found, as with all the previous attacks in this part of the 56th (London) Division's battlefield, that the unit on their left (part of the Guards) had not advanced in a similar fashion. This meant that the newly won position was 'in the air' on all flanks, and it was not long before bombing attacks from the direction of Morval forced the Middlesex back. By the end of the day the only gain was 50 yards of ground from the old front line from that afternoon. One officer had been killed,[8] nine were wounded (including both Tremlett and White) and one missing.[9] Other rank casualties were 155 killed, wounded and missing.

The 12th September was spent with the 1/8th holding the new positions, and the 1/7th behind; the latter losing two officers and fifty men from shell-fire around Wedge Wood. That evening the 1/7th were relieved by the 1st Buffs and 1/8th by the 8th Bedfordshires, both battalions moving back to Billon Copse.

An Obscure Position

As this next phase of the fighting came to a temporary close, the positions now held by the 56th (London) Division could only be called obscure. The divisional historian later remarked,

> ... We may say that the battalion reports of positions were only relatively accurate, and that nothing was clear to Gen. Hull until the weather improved and air reports could be made.[10]

Once the elements of 168th and 169th Brigades were relieved by units of the 5th Division around the 11th/12th September it was clear that positions at one time thought to be occupied were not. The infamous Quadrilateral, for example, was at one time reported reached, occupied and by-passed. It now transpired that it was still in German hands, as the Guards had found out, alongside the 1/8th Middlesex on the 12th. On this difficult left flank, where it joined another Division (in fact two different divisions in one week) the Quadrilateral was proving a major problem, a

> ... danger point, and it defied all attempts to take it by bombing, and successfully withstood the Corps heavy artillery.[11]

In the middle position around Bouleaux Wood the units there found themselves partially in the wood, and partially alongside. In some cases both sides' sets of trenches adjoined, divided only by a bomb block. The same was true on the right flank between Leuze Wood and the valley past Falfemont Farm. Here The Loop was still in dispute, but the wood was now occupied. The French had come up on the extreme right, but not far enough forward to outflank Combles itself.

It was clear that a new breakthrough, a fresh advance, was needed to clear this position and advance on and beyond Combles. At GHQ such plans were already in hand. Douglas Haig himself had seen a need to isolate Combles and ordered the now prepared elements of the Heavy Branch Machine Gun Corps forward to assist in the next infantry attack scheduled for 15th September. The dawn of the tanks had come.

1. Dudley Ward, C.H. The <u>56th Division</u> (John Murray 1921) p.63.

2. 2/Lt Tasso Scott Apergis, 10th attached 16th Londons, KIA 10.9.16 and 2/Lt Alexander Francis Johnston, 11 th attached 16th Londons, KIA 10.9.16. Both have no known grave and are commemorated on the Thiepval Memorial.

3. Henriques, J.Q., Major- <u>The War History of the 1st Battalion Queen's Westminster Rifles 1914-1918</u> (The Medici Society 1923) p.117.

4. Captain James William Long and 2/Lt Ernest William Lockey were killed, and the rest wounded. Long has no known grave and is commemorated on the Thiepval Memorial. Lockey is buried in Delville Wood Cemetery, Longueval.

5. Henriques op cit. p. 118.

6. Captain Alfred Horace MacGregor, KIA 19.9.16. No known grave -commemorated on the Thiepval Memorial.

7. 2/Lt Alan S.Petrie 14th Londons, KIA 10.9.16. 2/Lt George Thomson 9th Argyll & Sutherland Highlanders attached 14th Londons, KIA 10.9.16. Both are buried in Guillemont Road Cemetery.

8. 2/Lt E. H. Colcott 1/8th Middlesex Regiment, KIA 11.9.16. Buried Bray Military Cemetery.

9. 2/Lt W. J. MacDonnagh 1/8th Middlesex Regiment was originally posted as "believed wounded and evacuated through another regimental aid post" (War Diary PRO WO95/2950) but was later found to have been KIA 11.9.16. No known grave - commemorated on the Thiepval Memorial.

10. Dudley Ward op cit. p.65.

11. ibid. p.66.

Chapter Four

THE TANKS GO IN

The Battle of Flers-Courcelette, the official name eventually given to the action of 15th September 1916, was on a wide front, with Courcelette on the left, Flers roughly in the middle and the ground opposite Combles on the right. In between these locations were many other key positions; Martinpuich and High Wood among them. A total of eleven British, Canadian and New Zealand divisions were to advance at Zero Hour on the 15th, and supporting them for the first time in military history were more than 40 tanks of the Heavy Branch Machine Gun Corps (HB MGC). By this stage of the battle the creeping barrage was more commonplace, and earlier problems with 'drop shorts' - shells dropping short of the target and landing on the attacking troops - were beginning to be ironed out. Once again divisional artillery units allocated artillery liaison officers to accompany the battalions into action, to better co-ordinate the use of the guns on the battlefield, and enable the infantry to call back for

British troops in an assembly trench, September 1916.

protective fire if needed. Hopes were high for this next phase of the offensive, the objectives of which Douglas Haig saw as,

> ... to pivot on the high ground south of the Ancre and north of the Albert-Bapaume road, while the Fourth Army devoted its whole effort to the rearmost of the enemy's original systems of defence between Morval and Le Sars... I made arrangements to enable me to extend the left of the attack to embrace the villages of Martinpuich and Courcelette... Meanwhile our Allies arranged to continue the line of advance in close co-operation with me from the Somme to the slopes above Combles; but directed their main effort northwards against the villages of Rancourt and Frégicourt, so as to complete the isolation of Combles and open the way for their attack on Sailly-Saillisel.[1]

Hopes were indeed so high that advance units of the Cavalry Corps were kept in reserve at Carnoy, so that when the villages of Morval, LesBoeufs, Guedecourt and Flers were taken in the advance, the cavalry would move forward and capture the high ground beyond between Rocquigny, Villers au Flos, Riencourt and Bapaume.

56th (London) Division were again part of XIV Corps for this operation, which also consisted of the Guards and 6th Division. Fifteen tanks of the HB MGC were allocated to the Corps: nine to the Guards, three to the 6th and three to the 56th. The basic orders issued to the tanks were,

> ... to start their attack at a time which would enable them to reach the first objective five minutes before the infantry. When they had cleared up the first objective, a proportion of them was to push forward a short way, to prearranged positions, and act as strong points. Departure from this programme to assist any infantry held up by the enemy was left to the discretion of the tank commander.[2]

Once the second objective was reached, the HB MGC and the infantry units would advance together at a set rate - called 'tank pace' - which was deemed to be between 30 to 50 yards a minute. At the third and fourth objectives there could be no creeping barrage as the advance would have outstripped its field gun support, so once again the tanks would be required to move ahead of the infantry, clear up the objective, crush wire obstacles and suppress hostile rifle and machine-gun fire. To enable the infantry and tanks to communicate, coloured flags would be used with, for example, a red flag indicating 'out of action' and a green one 'am on objective'. This was the theory; and indeed the 56th (London) Division were one of the few formations in the Fourth Army to have undertaken training of this kind alongside the tanks. The reality would be very different.

The task of the XIV Corps on 15th September was to use the Guards and 6th Division to advance into the enemy line in strength, and clear the ground beyond Ginchy to enable the capture of Morval. 56th Division, on the extreme right flank, would also be required to advance on the enemy line, but one of its main tasks would be to lay down defensive posts around Combles to guard the join of the British and French lines. As such the Division's task in this operation would be finally to clear Bouleaux Wood, moving beyond it to protect the ground between Combles and Morval. This would be allocated to the 167th Brigade, who were to advance on the section of Beef Trench running through the wood and also take Middle Copse. Here the lines would join with the 6th Division on their left. 168th Brigade was then to advance through them and continue to the ground north of Combles beyond Bouleaux Wood. 169th Brigade on the right were to attack from Leuze Wood towards the sunken road running into Combles, capturing at the same time the troublesome position known as The Loop. To assist, two of the tanks of HB MGC would operate on the

Trench map showing the southern area of operations at Combles 15th September 1916. (PRO)

167th and 168th Brigade front, and the third would go in with the 169th at The Loop.

The weather was now beginning to play a factor in the outcome of some operations on the Somme, and by mid September the rains had come. The Divisional historian recorded that,

> ... the field of battle was a field of mud; the resting area of the division was a field of mud; the roads and tracks were rivers of mud; anyone can paint a picture of the Battle of the Somme provided that he can paint miles of mud. And the Army had simply blasted its way forward so that the shell holes cut one another in the mud.[3]

Because of this stretcher bearers were now having to operate eight men to one stretcher, and an ambulance required six horses to pull it in these conditions, as opposed to the usual two. Such conditions are often equated with the Battle of Passchendaele in 1917, and it is often forgotten that they prevailed on the Somme the year before.

The condition of the battlefield by this time was also truly appalling. Around Bouleaux Wood and Leuze Wood there had been little time for either side to bury the dead who had fallen in the fighting of early September. Bodies, and bits of bodies, covered the entire battlefield, and constant shelling re-interred the few who had been buried in shell holes or shallow graves. With shattered trees, and field after field of overlapping shell holes full of liquid mud, this moonscape covered with the smashed remains of those who had once fought over it had truly become a hell on earth.

Such were the conditions, the orders and the hopes that befell the 56th (London) Division as it approached some of the fiercest fighting in the entire history of the Division's experience on the Western Front.

The Attack of 167th Brigade

Operating on the left flank of the Division, the 167th Brigade had been ordered to advance on Beef Trench and Middle Copse, along the left side of Bouleaux Wood. In the vanguard of the attack was the 1/1st Londons (Royal Fusiliers), with the 1/7th Middlesex Regiment in reserve on the west side of Leuze Wood.

Commanded by Lieutenant Colonel D.V. Smith DSO, the 1/1st Londons placed C and D Companies in the front line to lead the attack, with B and A following in support. The four companies moved out at 5.50am on the 15th for Zero Hour at 6.20, and advanced on Beef Trench. Here they found that the preliminary bombardment had been ineffectual, and that '... the enemy trench was undamaged and fully manned'.[4] Wire entanglements untouched by the shells presented a great impassable barrier, and German machine-guns swept the ground in front of C and B Companies, causing heavy losses. By this time seven of the eight officers present were casualties, along with 75% of the men. D Company on the left were able to push forward a little way, and their No 16 Platoon captured Middle Copse via Gropi Trench. This position was consolidated, and a Lewis gun brought up. A Company had come through them and attempted to push on, but by nightfall had withdrawn as the battalion's flanks were badly in the air. Casualties were four officers killed[5] and seven wounded. Among the other ranks, 56 were killed, 136 wounded and 84 missing: however, *Soldiers Died indicates that 126 men from the battalion died in this attack.*[6] On the night of 15th/16th the battalion was reinforced by 14 officers and 104 men, who had moved up from Billon Farm. The next day consolidation of the position continued, and it proved possible to push a trench from C and D Companies in Bouleaux Wood to the sunken road that ran to Combles. During these operations Second Lieutenant L. St C. Dickinson, the battalion signals officer, was killed,[7] with six men also killed and 25 wounded. On the morning of the 17th the battalion was relieved by the 1/8th Middlesex.

The 1/7th Middlesex Regiment (Lieutenant Colonel E.J. King CMG) were in reserve when the 1/1st Londons went over, and as the morning progressed contact was lost with the assaulting battalion and it became increasingly unclear what was happening. The Middlesex advanced at 8.20 am, with the intention of passing through the Londons and clearing Bouleaux Wood. However, the leading waves were brought to a standstill by rifle fire from the front, and machine-gun fire to the right. The reserve companies came up, but suffered a similar fate, with the whole battalion now being pinned down and unable to advance. By this stage all four company commanders were hit: Captain Hurd of D Company had brought forward his Lewis guns in an attempt to lay down fire enabling the unit to advance. But he was mortally wounded in the head while personally directing the fire of his men.[8] By the afternoon the situation was unchanged and at 1pm the 1/8th Middlesex came up. Initially ordered to attack down the edge of Bouleaux Wood, these orders were changed and instead they dug in. At nightfall the 1/7th withdrew to the old front line in Bouleaux Wood, where they remained until relief the next day. Out of 500 men from the battalion who had gone into the attack, over 300 were casualties. One of the companies was reduced to only 25 men. In total nine officers were killed or died of wounds,[9] three wounded and one wounded and missing.[10] That famous luck of the 'Lucky Seventh' had finally run out.

Tanks on the 167th Brigade Front

Originally two tanks had been allocated to the 167th Brigade for this attack, but unfortunately one had broken down en-route. Both these tanks were from C Company HB MGC and had arrived at the railhead north of Bray, known as The Loop (not to be confused with the Loop at Leuze Wood) on 13th September. The two tanks, C13 and C14, were commanded by Lieutenant Sir John Dashwood and Second Lieutenant F.J.Arnold respectively. C13 was a male tank, armed with two six pounder guns, and C14 a female, armed with machine-guns. Dashwood was the unit's commander, and took the tanks from the railhead to Chimpanzee Valley, south of Trones Wood, on the 14th. From here they were allocated a guide who would take them up to the area of the front lines. The guide was Rifleman W.J. Gray of the 1/9th Londons (QVRs). He later recalled,

> ... the run between Brigade HQ and Battalion HQ would usually take something like twenty minutes, but owing to unsuitable ground a longer route had to be taken which should have been covered in about thirty minutes, but the tanks' capabilities in those early days were not as good as they subsequently became, and after a struggle of three hours and twenty minutes the first tank got into position a few yards behind our section of the line.[11]

Close to Angle Wood, Dashwood's C13 shed a track, which left Arnold's C14 to continue alone to the 167th Brigade sector. Crossing the Guillemont-Combles road, the tank commander noted the assembly trenches packed with troops waiting to go over, and then moved forward himself in the direction of Beef Trench.

The German unit opposite was the 28th Reserve Infantry Regiment, identified from the regimental account of the 1/1st Londons, who were virtually untouched by the preparatory bombardment. When they saw C14 coming through the smoke towards them, it was a confusing and worrying sight. No German soldier had ever seen a tank before, and some at first thought it some kind of threshing machine. Indeed, the provisional name given to the tank by the Germans was a "Panzerautoähnlicher Tank".[12] However, once Arnold gave the first order to open fire with his machine-guns, such innocent thoughts were soon cast aside.

The tank reached Beef Trench, but despite this the German defenders were able to lay down a withering fire on the 1/1st Londons as they approached the objective. Their attack soon dwindled (see above). Arnold in C14 continued with his advance and moved into the open ground between Middle Copse and Bouleaux Wood. Here the tank moved round and round, firing on any targets that presented itself. While the commander of 1/1st Londons might have wished to have the tank back again and assist him at Beef Trench and Middle Copse, Arnold followed his last minute updated orders which had dictated that he should move towards Morval and destroy any wire that might hinder the advance of the 6th Division. Instead,

> ... the tank moved down the north-west edge of Bouleaux Wood and reached a point within a very short distance of the northern end. He [Arnold] did a lot of execution when he hit the German front but unfortunately he did not wait for the infantry to consolidate the point that he was dominating... Having shot up the Huns on their front line he immediately proceeded to attack Germany all on his own. He moved down the edge of Bouleaux Wood shooting at every living thing he saw... Finding that no infantry were following him, he returned to find out what had happened to them.[13]

This report comes from the commanding officer of C Company HB MGC, Allen Holford-Walker. In it he also claims that Arnold at one point was only a short distance from Morval itself but, given the failure of the 6th Division attack on the left, this seems unlikely.

Whatever, at one point Arnold was back near Beef Trench and it was in a large shell hole here that the tank ditched and became stuck. The crew went outside to try and dig it out, but came under a bombing attack by the Germans. It was then that Corporal Pattinson was killed,

Second Lieutenant Arnold's C14 tank, ditched in a shell hole alongside Bouleaux Wood. Morval is ahead on the skyline and the shattered nature of the ground is obvious. (IWM Q.49249)

attempting to throw back one of the bombs which had pitched over.[14] Two others engaged the enemy, and then retreated back inside the tank. Arnold went to the nearest infantry he could find to ask assistance, but it soon became clear that nothing could be done and so the weapons were sabotaged before the tank was finally abandoned. The crew made their way back to the British lines, and stumbled into the positions of the 8th Bedfordshires. By this time one had been killed coming back, and three were wounded.[15] Two men from the crew were later awarded the Military Medal. Arnold was awarded the Military Cross.

Outcome of 167th Brigade's Attack

In the original planning, the 168th Brigade was meant to come up through the 167th and continue to the high ground beyond Bouleaux Wood and north of Combles. Given the outcome of the day's fighting, and the inability even of tank C14 to reach Morval, this was not possible. Instead elements of the 168th came forward and occupied the positions being evacuated by the 167th Brigade. The Divisional historian had seen this left flank as the most difficult part of the battlefield before the 56th Division, stating,

> ... [the] Germans deserve the highest praise. They were of the

German artillery shelter at Combles, latterly used by machine-guns, September 1916. (IWM Q.4312)

21st and 7th Bavarian Regts of the 5th Bavarian Division. They were well wired in, and had in the Quadrilateral deep dugouts in their front lines and others in the ravine behind the position. But though we grant them a perfect position and well constructed defences, we must also admit they performed a fine feat of arms. Those in the Quadrilateral resisted all efforts of the 56th and Guards Divisions to bomb them out... They had actually been under severe artillery fire and subjected to repeat assaults since the 9th September, and on the 15th, in spite of tanks, of creeping barrages, and of the heavy artillery, they remained immovable.[16]

Attack of the 169th Brigade

On the right flank, Brigadier General E.S.D'E. Coke's 169th Brigade were poised to take their part in the next phase of operations. Their task involved advancing across the Combles ravine to try and finally secure Loop Trench, which had previously caused so many problems and, indeed, casualties. The French Army would be attacking on their immediate right flank, and it was hoped to maintain communications with them as the advance moved forward to Combles.

The leading battalion in the attack was 1/2nd London, still commanded by Lieutenant Colonel Attenborough. Zero Hour was 6.20am and the 1/2nd would attack in four waves with Captain A.G.L. Jepson's D Company in the first two, and Lieutenant J.H. Clive's C Company in the final two. A and B Companies, now amalgamated due to casualties from the earlier operations, were in reserve at Leuzenake Trench. The immediate objective was Loop Trench itself, but to reach it a complicated manoeuvre was planned whereby the waves would have to change direction to 'hug' the contours of the ground, thus avoiding fire from the strong points located in the sunken Combles road. In the event, this change of direction was achieved and the 1/2nd soon gained a foothold in Loop Trench. Fierce fighting followed, and the battalion edged towards the sunken road until bomb blocks in the trenches and uncut wire above ground stopped the advance. This gave the Germans a chance to counter-attack, and a bombing attack was sent forward to dislodge the 1/2nd Londons. Reinforcements from the reserve were sent up, and in the fight that followed the new ground gained was held but casualties were high - among them Captain Jepson commanding the first wave.[17]

But the German bombers kept coming forward, with seemingly endless salvos of stick grenades, or 'potato mashers' as the British troops called them, along with egg grenades and Kugel grenades, both

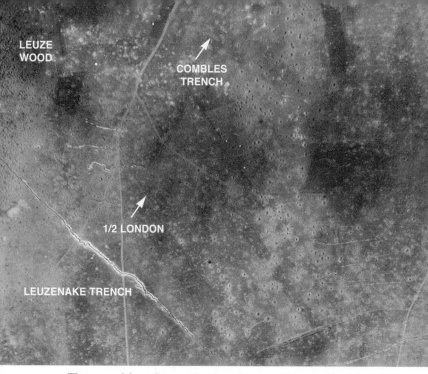

The ground from Leuzenake Trench over which 1/2nd Londons advanced on 15th September 1916. (IWM)

forms of fragmentation bombs. The losses among the 1/2nd bombers were so high that Lieutenant Colonel Attenborough was forced to call upon Lieutenant Colonel Husey MC's bombers in the London Rifle Brigade. These were duly sent up and forty-three men joined the 1/2nd at The Loop. Few of them returned. In addition two Stokes Mortars under Second Lieutenant A.J. Whittle also joined the fray, but despite heavy fighting the junction of The Loop and the sunken road remained in German hands.

With only subalterns left on the battlefield, Captain J.P. Kellet MC (who had only just rejoined the battalion) was sent up to take command. He arrived at The Loop in the early afternoon of the 15th September and reported back to headquarters,

> ... *The battalion bombers have established a block at the junction of 'V' Trench (Loop Trench) and Loop... The artillery have again shortened their range on sunken road and have wounded two more bombers. The line appears to me to be far too thinly held. The hostile attack fizzled out.*[18]

Due to the heavy shelling, the trenches were now in a poor state, and offered little protection from both shell and machine-gun fire. German

British troops move forward to the attack, September 1916.

snipers were also active, and again the poor state of the line meant they were given numerous easy targets. Captain Kellett allocated a group to each of the main parts of the new positions and set about improving the defences at the bombing blocks and deepening the trenches, adding fire steps where possible. This work was completed by the evening, and under cover of darkness the beleaguered defenders of The Loop were much cheered by the arrival of post from England and hot food from the battalion cookers. At the same time one of the London Field Companies of the Royal Engineers, and a detachment from the 1/5th Cheshires, came up and constructed a new strong point around The Loop. By the end of the day, "... the position, therefore, could be regarded as far more satisfactory".[19]

At 11am a further attack, using the LRB bombing section, was made against the sunken road, under Second Lieutenant St Ledger of 1/2nd Londons. Once again this operation was not successful, but Brigadier General Coke was determined to breach the defences here and sent down a further order that another attempt was to be made at 5 am on the 16th. At this hour Second Lieutenant St Ledger went out again with his bombers, but again came under withering fire. St Ledger was killed by small arms fire,[20] and his bombing Sergeant, Sergeant Bullock,[21] was killed in a bombing fight. The few survivors returned to The Loop.

Captain Kellett was later to call this a "trying night", and in the early hours of the 16th September he found that the line he held was now garrisoned by seven officers, thirteen battalion bombers, forty-four men from A Company, eighty-one from B, forty-five from C and thirty-one from D. In addition there were seventeen men from the LRB bombing section left, twelve Stokes Mortar personnel and fourteen machine-gunners of the 169th Company MGC. With at least a battalion strength German formation in front of him, Kellett realised that this was not favourable odds, and if the Germans counter-attacked again under cover of a good bombardment then it was unlikely his men could hold. To make matters worse, the garrison had been heavily shelled by British 8-inch howitzers consistently, causing casualties and the destruction of a bombing block between The Loop and Combles Trench. Kellett had signalled back to Lieutenant Colonel Attenborough, who had tried to stop  this, but it proved impossible to find out which battery was firing o▪ this area. The men were worn out from the combat, from lack of slee▪ and constant harassment from the enemy. Kellett sat in his trench an▪ no doubt wondered what the future held. Luckily for him no Germa▪ attack came on the 16th, or the night of the 16th/17th and he was abl▪ to hand over the position to the LRB intact.

The 1/2nd Londons moved back to Falfemont Farm, where it wa▪ determined that four officers and 10 other ranks were killed, thre▪ officers and 19 other ranks wounded and 251 other ranks missing▪ Captain Kellett received no immediate award for his bravery ▪▪ Combles, but was awarded the DSO and bar in 1918, and rose t▪ command the battalion by the end of the war. He survived the Grea▪ War.

Tanks on the 169th Brigade Front

Only one tank was allocated to the 169th Brigade for the fighting ▪▪ The Loop. This was tank C16, commanded by Second Lieutenant Eri▪ Purdy. C16, tank No 510, was a female armed with two sponson▪ carrying twin Vickers machine-guns. Like the other tanks allotted t▪ the 56th Division, it came up via the railhead at The Loop and the▪

C16, a tank commanded by Second Lieutenant Purdy, after it shed a track near Leuze Wood on 15th September 1916. (IWM Q.49248)

crossed to Chimpanzee Valley before moving up to the battlefield. Here Purdy took the tank into Leuze Wood, along what was left of a pre-war ride through the trees. This afforded some protection from observation from the German lines on the other side of the wood. Here he waited until Zero Hour.

At 6am Purdy moved the tank out, and it came round the south edge of Leuze Wood, heading towards The Loop. In doing so his objective was to assist the 1/2nd Londons in their own advance on this position. There were few landmarks left on the battlefield at this stage, with all the shelling, and it was difficult for Purdy and his driver to find the correct route to the objective. However, he managed to reach the area of The Loop and lay down fire from the Vickers guns. The German machine-gunners responded, but realising their weapons were not having any effect, they changed target and fired on the 1/2nd Londons as they started their advance. It was at this point Purdy was able to silence these weapons and assist the Londons attack.

As the advance continued, shelling from both sides got heavier.

A rear view of C16 following the capture of Combles showing that, aside from the track problem, the rest of the tank was intact. (Norman Date)

During the winter of 1916/17 several French photographers visited C16. Here it is shown in the snow, with Leuze Wood barely recognisable behind the tank. (Norman Date)

Somewhere between The Loop and Combles Trench the tank was struck by a shell - possibly a British 'drop short' from the creeping barrage - and came to a halt, shedding a track. It proved impossible to get the machine going again, and although Purdy was able to lay down further covering and direct fire for a while, his ammunition ran out and the Germans threatened his position, so he gave orders to abandon the tank and set it on fire. Purdy was eventually awarded a Military Cross for his bravery in this action. However, what he and his men never knew was that a German patrol entered the tank some time later and found the personal diary of one of the crew, which gave them vital intelligence information about the tank and the training for the crews. It is preserved in the Bavarian Archives at Munich.[22]

This tank's contribution to the fighting for The Loop can therefore, at best, be called limited. In retrospect it is surprising that a female tank was allocated for this attack, when it is clear that a tank armed with 6-pounder guns could have done far more destruction to The Loop. Reactions among the men of the 56th Division was varied. In the QWR they felt "... the tank had served some useful purpose".[23] Aubrey Smith of the LRB observed, "... the Germans had certainly been terrified by them",[24] but the historian of the 56th Division later concluded,

> ... in the XIV Corps area the tanks were by no means a success. It is only right to say this was not the fault of their crews. Every excuse must be allowed, for the tank was not only a new invention, and, like most new inventions, somewhat clumsy in the first design, but the ground was absolutely vile.[25]

It was clear among the men of the London division that the day of the tank was yet to come, and they would indeed be there to witness it at Cambrai in November 1917, and in the key battles of the Hundred Days in 1918.

The Fighting Continues

The shattered battalions of the 167th and 169th Brigades who had participated in the fighting of 15th September were gradually relieved in the front line and replaced by others who had greater strength and had been in reserve. Plans were already in hand to continue with the advance around Combles, and Major General Hull put in operation instructions for the fighting to continue on the 18th September. The 17th was therefore spent in preparing for this new assault.

The advance on the 18th was a joint operation with the 6th Division on the left. The Quadrilateral was still causing problems, and remained in German hands, and the 6th would finally attempt to clear it. The London troops would, on the right, attempt to reach the positions in the sunken road to Combles, and on the left capture the south-west face of Bouleaux Wood at a point just beyond Beef Trench, and move on to Middle Copse. Here the 56th would meet up with the 6th. Given the problems of tanks in the operations of the 15th, both divisions refused the assistance of them on this occasion.

Zero Hour was 5.50 am, and on the right flank two battalions would advance: the QWR and the LRB. On the front of the Queen's Westminsters a series of assembly trenches had been prepared by the 1/5th Cheshires and a handful of 1/2nd Londons. Approximately parallel with the objective, the strong points beyond The Loop at the sunken road, the battalion moved into them around 4.30 am. The attack would be supported by a heavy bombardment and a Stokes Mortar barrage onto the remains of the Orchard that ran along the northern edge of the sunken road as it came into Combles. Two machine-guns from 169th Company MGC were attached to the QWR to consolidate

The sunken lane near The Orchard, looking towards Leuze Wood, as it is today.

British troops and German prisoners cross the battlefield under fire.

the objective once it was taken. The LRB would also be advancing on the right flank of the battalion. Due to the losses sustained in earlier battles around Combles, the battalion could only muster three reduced strength companies for this attack. No 2 Company (elements of B and D) went over on the right, commanded by Captain J.A. Green. On the left was Captain M.M. Webb's No 1 Company (old A) and in support was No 3, where Second Lieutenant N.T. Thurston had the remnants of the old C Company.

At 5.50 am No 1 and No 2 Companies left the assembly trenches and walked straight into an enemy barrage, which seemed to open almost at once. However, the men pushed on and had almost reached the objective when they came under heavy machine-gun fire, which virtually stopped the battalion in its tracks. A handful of men had got to the sunken road at one point, and Second Lieutenant E. Jones reached the German trench with a sergeant, only to be shot down while encouraging his platoon forward.[26] It was now clear the enemy was holding this position in strength, and as the losses in the two assaulting companies had been so heavy, it was not possible to continue. Second Lieutenant Thurston had brought the support company into the assembly trenches shortly after Zero, anticipating their need. However, he had come under heavy shell fire and was ordered to hold his ground until further orders arrived. As early as 6.45am it was realised in a message to battalion headquarters that,

> ... *the first line nearly to objective, and then wiped out. Only twenty left of assaulting company and about fifty of support company. Impossible to advance over the open.*[27]

Thus by late morning the QWR had been reduced to a mere three officers and ninety men. These were clinging to the assembly trenches in the pouring rain, supported by the two Vickers guns from 169th MGC. The advance had ended.

Losses in the QWR were severe. In a much reduced battalion, more than a hundred had been killed or wounded. All the officers in A Company were dead, among them Captain Webb who had initially been wounded, and then later killed near the sunken road.[28] Some good news did arrive at Lieutenant Colonel Shoolbred's headquarters the next day when it was found that over seventy men had been lying in shell holes around the German positions and had come back in under cover of darkness. This brought the unit's strength up to 160 all ranks; at the same time a draft of 180 arrived from the base. It was found that these men had less than twelve weeks military service, and no overseas experience.

On the right the London Rifle Brigade made their advance. Following alongside the QWR the now famed LRB bombers captured 200 yards of trench in the initial phase of the operation. This piece of trench ran into the sunken road, and despite German counter attacks from the direction of the Orchard, this trench was held. Casualties in the LRB were not as heavy as in the QWR, who had born the brunt of the fighting. On the night of the 18th the LRB took over the assembly trenches now vacated by the QWR, as well as part of The Loop.

Over on the left flank, the London Scottish had been ordered to attack alongside 6th Division. Supporting them were the 1/4th Londons, and the objective involved the advance already described near Beef Trench, Middle Copse and Leuze Wood. Both units were at Angle Wood when the orders arrived, and instructions were given that the two battalions would need to be at the north-west corner of Leuze Wood (dead ground which was out of view of the Germans) by 4 am on the 18th. Here a Brigade Major would meet them both and lead them up to the assembly point for the attack. This sounded easy on paper, but the weather had broken by this point and rain had turned the battlefield into a quagmire. The battalion historian recalls that the London Scottish reached the corner of the wood with minutes to spare after a "superhuman exertion" on the part of all ranks. However, 1/4th had not come up in time. The officer commanding the London Scottish suggested an attack without the Fusiliers, and this was eventually agreed to. However, by this time the Brigade Major could not get the attackers into the assembly positions before dawn, by which time they would be seen by the Germans and no doubt subjected to heavy punishment. He decided, wisely, to abort the attack.

Once again the advance on the Quadrilateral had floundered. Once again Bouleaux Wood and even parts of Leuze Wood were still in the hands of German units, who appeared to be in strength. It would need one last effort on the part of the men of the 56th (London) Division to achieve what had been laid before them almost three weeks before. The ground at Combles had become a mincing machine, slowly wearing the Division down. The balance must now be redressed.

1. Douglas Haig's dispatch quoted in Dudley Ward, C.H. The 56th Division (John Murray 1921)p.68-69.
2. ibid. p.70.
3. ibid. p.72.
4. 1/1st Londons War Diary PRO WO95/2949.
5. Officers killed: Lieut J.D. Fry, 2/Lt G.S. Hill, 2/Lt S.F. Snowden and 2/Lt E.W. Sheasby. Fry is buried in Combles Communal Cemetery Extension; the others are

commemorated on the Thiepval Memorial.

6. Soldiers Died In The Great War 1914-19 CD ROM (Naval and Military Press 1998)

7. 2/Lt Lionel St Clair Dickinson, 1/1st Londons, KIA 16.9.16. Buried in Combles Communal Cemetery Extension.

8. Captain Douglas William Hurd, 1/7th Middlesex, DOW 17.9.16. Buried Bronfay Farm Military Cemetery.

9. The killed officers killed or died of wounds were: 2/Lt H.L. Cooper, Capt H.W. Hanbury, Capt D.W. Hurd, 2/Lt G.H.W. Taylor, Capt J.K. Tully, 2/Lt Westoby (attached 167th MGC), 2/Lt J.E. Whitehead, 2/Lt A. Whyman, and Capt W.G. Woodroffe. Cooper, Hanbury, Taylor, Westoby, Whitehead and Whyman are all buried in Combles Communal Cemetery Extension. Hurd and Woodroffe are in Bronfay Farm Cemetery. Tully is buried in Corbie Communal Cemetery Extension.

10. 2/Lt P.H. Rowe, 1/7th Middlesex, DOW 17.9.16. Rowe seems to have been buried by the Germans, as initially he was posted missing and erroneously commemorated on the Arras Memorial. At some time in the 1920s or 30s his body was found, and he is now buried at Serre Road No 2 Cemetery.

11. Cuthbert Keeson, C.A. The History & Records of Queen Victoria's Rifles 1792-1922 (Constable 1923) p.190ff.

12. Quoted in Miles, W. Military Operations France and Belgium 1916 Vol 2 (Macmillan and Co 1938) p.309.

13. PRO CAB45.

14. Cpl G.E. Pattinson, C Coy HB MGC, KIA 15.9.16. Buried Combles Cemetery Extension.

15. The soldier who was killed is Gnr (Pte) B.A.Giles, C Coy HB MGC, KIA 15.9.16.

16. Dudley Ward op cit. p.73-74.

17. Captain A.G.L. Jepson, 1/2nd Londons, KIA 15.9.16. Commemorated Thiepval Memorial. Jepson joined the battalion in August 1914, and was wounded at Hooge a year later in 1915. He was mentioned in despatches in January 1916.

18. Grey, W.E. The 2nd City of London Regiment (Royal Fusiliers) In The Great War 1914-19 (By The Regiment 1929) p.139.

19. ibid.

20. 2/Lt St J. R. St Ledger, 1/2nd Londons, KIA 16.9.16. Commemorated Thiepval Memorial. Born in 1885, St Ledger had previously served in both the Leinster Regiment and Bedfordshire Regiment, joining the 1/2nd in July 1915.

21. Sgt A.E.A. Bullock, 1/2nd Londons, KIA 16.9.16. Born Knightsbridge, living in Wandsworth.

22. This document is reproduced in Pidgeon, T. The Tanks At Flers (By the author). Further detailed information on all the tanks at Combles can be found in this book.

23. Henriques, J.Q. The War History of the 1st Battalion Queen's Westminster Rifles 1914-1918 (Medici Society 1923) p.119.

24. Smith, A. Four Years On The Western Front (Odhams 1922) p.176.

25. Dudley Ward op cit. p.71.

26. 2/Lt E.A.O. Jones, 1/16th Londons (QWR), KIA 18.9.16. Commemorated Thiepval Memorial. Jones' father had previously served with the regiment, and he himself as a private in the HAC in 1914.

27. Henriques op cit. p.122.

28. Captain M.M. Webb, 1/16th Londons (QWR), KIA 18.9.16. Buried Combles Cemetery Extension. It was said of him he was, " an outstanding example of the many young officers who fulfilled responsibilities of command far beyond their years, and yet retained all the high spirits and light-heartedness of youth."

Chapter Five

THE CAPTURE OF COMBLES

The Fighting Goes On... And On
　　While plans for the next phase of operations on the Somme were being prepared, the men of the 56th (London) Division were still in the thick of the fighting around Bouleaux and Leuze Woods. Following the attack on the 18th September, over the next few days the Germans launched localised counter-attacks at various points east of Leuze Wood, but these were all beaten back. The London Scottish, not having taken part in the fighting on the 18th, remained in the line and loaned men as working parties to the 1/5th Cheshires (divisional pioneers) who worked on the trench systems - particularly around The Loop. This included putting in a trench from the knocked out tank, C16, to the main British line - thus turning the wreck of the vehicle into a static pillbox. However, it continued to draw fire from German guns and was probably ignored by the infantry. The Kensingtons came back into the line and took over trenches between Bouleaux Wood and Leuze Wood: here the rain cascaded down on the positions among the shattered

German map showing the situation after the Battle of Flers-Courcelette.
(Marcus Massing)

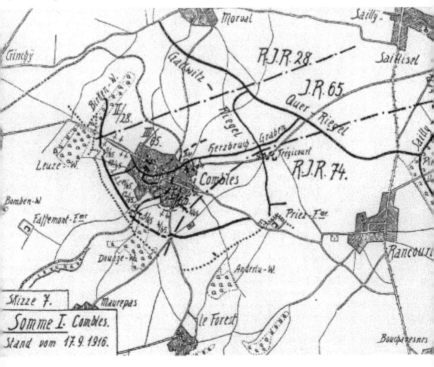

In a reserve trench during the Battle of Morval, September 1916.

trees, turning the smashed ground and Somme mud into even more of a mire. Because of these conditions, on the night the Kensingtons were relieved it took nearly ten hours to move back to the rest area at Maltzhorn Farm - nearly three times as long as normal.

One final operation took place before the last 'Big Push'. This was on 24th September when the QVRs bombed their way down Combles Trench in an effort to link up with the 73rd Regiment of Infantry (RI) of the French Army on their right. Initially doing well, the battalion floundered and German counter-attacks threw them back and they were not able to make touch with 73rd RI. The QVRs had received a draft of over 300 new men a few days previously, none of which had seen action before and most of them had only been in the army twelve weeks. This was a great problem with drafts to infantry units at this time: it was in fact only a matter of weeks before the first conscripts arrived on the battlefield. Their standard of training was often found to be well below what was expected for a front line battalion.

The Beginning Of The End - 25th September 1916

Since the Battle of Flers-Courcelette on 15th September, the situation on the right flank of the Fourth Army, where it joined the French, had been less than satisfactory. The divisions involved in the fighting there - including, of course, the 56th - had been unable to clear the ground as expected. This was largely due to the dominant position of the Quadrilateral on the road to Morval, and the difficult positions held by the London battalions around the two woods. The next phase of attack was being planned, and would involve an advance which would encompass Guedecourt on the left, LesBoeufs and Morval in the centre, and Combles on the right. The attack would be in conjunction with the French, who would attack at the same time - 12.35 pm on the 25th September. This was a Zero Hour dictated by the French and,

Over the top! British soldiers advance during the Battle of Morval, 25th September 1916.

considering that most of the previous September operations on Fourth Army front had been at or before dawn, it was a distinct change. The French, however, were not happy about attacking in half light, and claimed that their troops were not sufficiently trained to do it. Given the outcome of this sort of timing on the 1st July, Rawlinson and his subordinates at Fourth Army were no doubt anxious about this new arrangement.

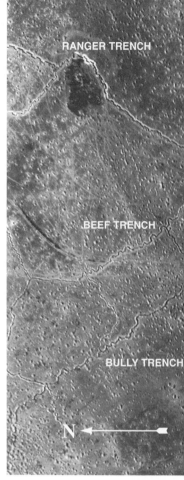

The XIV Corps, of which 56th (London) Division was still a part, was allocated to attack on a frontage opposite Morval across to Combles. The 5th and 6th Division would spearhead the advance, supported by a concentrated barrage with a high proportion of heavy guns, and a number of tanks would be attached to them. Some days before a staff meeting at Fourth Army headquarters had expressed concerns about the possible performance of the tanks, given the worsening state of the ground. There were greater worries over being able to conceal their movement on the way up to the assembly points: there being no cover left in this part of the battlefield. However, several were eventually allotted to the XIV Corps as the approach area – with valleys and dead ground – was arguably more suitable.

The 56th Division's role in these operations was to "safeguard the right flank of the army". To do so they would use additional artillery, Stokes Mortars and machine-guns to neutralise the Germans in the area of Bouleaux Wood and the approaches to Combles. A smoke barrage was also to be placed in front of the assaulting battalions, as the attack would be in daylight. Major General Hull, commanding the 56th, was given direct contact with the French 2nd Division on his right in an attempt to enable both formations finally to capture the

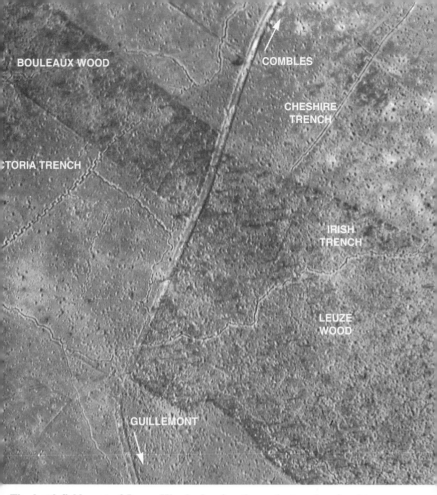

The battlefield west of Leuze Wood, showing the main trenches fought over in September 1916. (IWM)

village of Combles. This main attack would not take place on the 25th, but wait until the 26th and the outcome of other operations on the XIV Corps frontage.

The 25th September broke with fine weather, sunny in places and a little bit of haze. This was in marked contrast to the appalling weather of the past few weeks. It boded well for the outcome of the operation. Shelling increased on the German positions that morning until 12.35pm, Zero Hour, when a powerful creeping barrage was laid 200 yards in front of the British lines as the attacking battalions went 'over the top'. For once, the artillery was doing its job and,

> *... for the most part the Germans who had survived the bombardment were caught before they were prepared for*

resistance; some even fled unarmed. The enemy defensive barrage generally fell too late, and British casualties, except in a few units, were by no means heavy. It was a heartening experience, a success well deserved by four divisions which, since the beginning of the month, had given repeated proof of their gallantry and endurance, too often with little reward.[1]

On the 56th Division front only the units of the 168th Brigade took part; the others waiting for the planned joint advance with the French. The two assaulting battalions were 1/4th Londons and London Scottish, who had been allocated to attack on the 18th when that operation had been cancelled. These two battalions were on the left flank of the Division, with 5th Division on their left and Bouleaux Wood as the main objective.

1/4th Londons were on the right. They advanced at 12.35 pm with two companies in the first wave. The first objective was soon reached, following closely behind the smoke and the creeping barrage, and the battalion,

... killed a large number of Huns in shell-holes round the north end of the wood, and suffered somewhat from enemy snipers in the southern part of the wood.[2]

The final objective was reached as early as 1.15pm. Later on patrols went in to clear Bouleaux Wood, and parties of Royal Engineers and 1/5th Cheshires came up to establish strong points in the new line. A further strong point was established on the embankment north of the wood, this line now forming part of a salient as Morval was now in British hands. Casualties in the 1/4th were light, with one officer killed, six other ranks dead and only a handful of wounded.

The London Scottish went over on the left, adjoining the 5th Division. While 1/4th Londons were occupying the enemy in Bouleaux Wood, the battalion would advance to their objective, the trench running from the north-east corner of the wood to a strong point on the light railway (blasted away by shell fire) that ran to Morval. A and C Companies went over in the first wave, with A detailed to take the strong point and C the trench. B Company was behind in support, while D was in reserve. It was decided to make Zero Hour 2 pm, giving time for other units in the XIV Corps to have made their advance successfully.

The leading platoons left their assembly line promptly at 2 pm. In fact one was so eager it advanced a little too early and ran into its own creeping barrage. Captain Worlock's C Company took the trench allocated to them fairly easily. Another trench, not noted in intelligence

When the patrols of 56th (London) Division entered Combles, the village had already been utterly wrecked by shell fire.

reports, was found nearby and Worlock was able to capture that as well. Lieutenant Speak and A Company ran into trouble at the strong point, which they found well protected by barbed wire. A bombing fight ensued, the company now pinned down. Speak called for the support company, but it had just lost its commander, Captain McLellan,[3] and second in command, Captain Wilson,[4] and were unable to come up for the moment. Speak kept pressing home the attack, and was awaiting the reserves to come up when he was wounded. However, almost at the same time he was able to witness the Germans surrendering, and the position was taken. In this one location three German officers, forty-nine men, three machine guns and four trench mortars were taken by Speak's company. The battalion was now able to make contact with elements of the 5th Division, advancing on Morval and, with the 1/4th

Combles railway station where 1/2nd and 1/5th Londons dug-in on the final objective, 26th September 1916.

Londons on the right, Bouleaux Wood was now all but cleared. During this operation the London Scottish had lost four officers and fifty men: a small price for much gain, and a distinct contrast from earlier operations in the area.

Combles Falls – 26th September 1916

With the distinct success of the other divisions in XIV Corps, and the capture of the line from LesBoeufs to Morval, the way was now open for the final assault on Combles. And with the French pushing hard on the right flank, it now seemed assured that victory was close. The final attack would have to clear what remained of Bouleaux Wood and Combles Trench, and the sunken road into Combles would have to fall, and then the village could be entered.

Combles itself was finally entered at 3.30 am on the 26th September. A mixed patrol of 1/2nd Londons and London Rifle

The remains of the church following the capture of Combles. Nearest the camera is a sandbagged entrance to the catacombs. (IWM Q.6220)

Brigade had the honour of being the first London troops in. The 1/2nd Londons were a combined force of the much reduced A and C Companies, commanded by Captain Kellett, who distinguished himself in previous operations. As Kellett led his men in, he noticed the LRB coming up on his left, and a French unit on the immediate right. He reported back at once to his battalion headquarters,

> ... A and C Companies have occupied Tranchée de Combles. A Company is now easing off to its left to get into its proper position. The LRB have searched right through the village and report all clear. They are now moving forward to trench along

French troops in occupation of the entrance to the cellar of Combles town hall.

Kellett rounded up a large number of wounded Germans left behind in the evacuation and a substantial amount of weaponry and ammunition was also taken. Continuing with the success, Kellett led the two companies on through Combles to the railway line north-east of the village. Here the men established a line among some old gun pits, which it was not possible to connect up due to the heavy shelling. The 1/1st Londons came up behind them and the line was held until relief on the night of the 26th. Casualties for this final operation had been 7 other ranks killed, and 51 wounded.

The London Rifle Brigade, meanwhile, were coming up on the left of 1/2nd Londons. A patrol under Second Lieutenant H.J. Simon of B Company pushed through the Loop at around 2.30am, and climbing up over the bomb block that separated one side from another, continued on into the sunken road. Here a group of five Germans were encountered and overcome, Simon's men taking a machine-gun at the same time. They pushed on further to the north-west of the village where their advance came to a halt opposite a trench strongly held by the enemy. LRB's A Company then came up and bombed their way into the position while, to the south, French troops were doing the same. Both forces met at around 3.30 am, as the Germans began to retire. A patrol from B Company then entered Combles, taking

200 prisoners. These were handed over to the French, as recent losses meant that all companies were well under strength and men could not be spared for prisoner escort duties. By 9.30 am the whole battalion was in the village, and the advance continued to a position 1,100 yards east of Combles. Here a new trench was found to be held by fresh German troops and Lieutenant Colonel Husey, commanding LRB, realised that he would not be able to take it without proper artillery support. Having advanced so far he had outrun the divisional artillery, and so would have to stay put for the moment. As his men cleared the village they found: 1,800 rifles, 8,500 bombs, three 76mm

View of Combles and the quarry, following the capture of the village by 56th (London) Division.

A French ration cart passing through the ruins of Combles.

Minnenwerfers (small trench mortars) and three flame throwers. One of these was a large one having been cemented into the basement of one of the houses. Examining its war booty, here the LRB stayed until relief on the 27th.

The 1/1st Londons were occupying a position from the south-west end of Bouleaux Wood to the north-east corner of Leuze Wood. Here they overlooked the sunken road which approached the village. On the morning of the 26th it was noted that the Germans sent up red rockets from their forward area, followed by a single green one. A patrol from C Company went ahead in the darkness, and found the sunken road and nearby Stew Trench empty. Pushing on they entered the Orchard, and here awaited further orders. A, B and D Companies then pushed through, with two platoons clearing the east side of Bouleaux Wood and entering Bystander Trench. At 7 am the Germans blew an ammunition store on the outskirts of Combles, and the battalion pushed on, soon meeting up with French troops near the railway line. 1/2nd Londons and the LRB were also close by. From here A and B Companies went on and occupied a line north-east of the village, encountering elements of the British 5th Division on their left. These positions were handed over to the 1/3rd Londons on the afternoon of the 26th. In the fighting the 1/1st had lost one officer wounded, with eight other ranks also wounded, and two missing.

One final operation, meanwhile, was being planned. At 2 pm the

Rangers were ordered to attack the German third line near Morval, close to where the 5th Division boundary met the 56th. Two tanks were brought up to assist, and were ordered to come up through Leuze Wood and attack the objective from the south. The Rangers put two companies in the sunken road west of Morval, with another two companies behind in support. The tanks came up, but soon ran into problems as the continued rain made the ground even more boggy. One got stuck on the Combles-Morval road, and the other returned to Leuze Wood, not attempting to reach the main objective of Mutton Trench. The Rangers were therefore ordered not to go over, but had to stand-to for the next twenty four hours while a further five tanks were mustered to come up and assist. None of these arrived, and 168th Brigade headquarters finally cancelled the operation on 27th September.[6]

The French Attack

Space sadly precludes any detailed account of the French operations around Combles. Indeed, these are worthy of a book in their own right. For the final attack on 25th-26th September, it was units from General Fayolle's Sixth Army that took part. Fayolle asked Foch for further support for the forthcoming attack and received extra heavy artillery transferred from the Verdun front, as well as an additional French air force squadron.

In the fighting for Combles French patrols entered the area around the village on the night of 25th/26th September. By dawn the 110th Regiment of Infantry (RI) had cleared the south-east area, and had taken over 200 prisoners. The 73rd RI came in from the south-west and joined up with men from the 56th (London) Division. Once Combles was secure, the French pushed on to Frégicourt and Fayolle ordered a second main attack to move forward on St Pierre Vaast Wood. This went in at 4 pm on the 26th, but was only partially successful. Here their line remained until the fighting of October 1916 as "... General Fayolle then decided that nothing more could be done without thorough artillery preparation".[7]

Conclusions

Combles had finally fallen around 3.30 am on 26th September 1916 – largely without a fight. Within a few days the forward units of 56th (London) Division were relieved and went into rest around Ville-sur-Ancre and Méaulte. The London battalions had paid a mighty price for the three weeks of fighting leading up to the capture of the village. Bouleaux Wood, by now known as 'Bully Wood', and Leuze Wood, or

Combles after the war.

157. COMBLES VILLAGE.

'Lousy Wood' had become the killing ground for hundreds of men from every battalion of the Division. The divisional historian concluded,

> *... this grim, determined, and desperate struggle revealed qualities in the London troops which, though they existed, would not in a more spectacular success have been so clearly demonstrated. It requires good men to attack again and again until their object is gained, and when these attacks are launched against such splendidly trained soldiers as the Germans, one can only marvel that the thing was ever done, and applaud the steadfast courage, the endurance of body and spirit, which enabled the men to do it.*[8]

Private A Stuart Dolden of the London Scottish, like many veterans of the fighting at Combles, saw things a little differently.

> *We were all filled with unbounding joy when we realised that at last our backs had been turned on the Somme, and all its horrors and miseries. The one outstanding feature of the Somme was the mud. Living with it around one, day and night, seemed to tap one's vitality. We had already experienced severe shelling, trenches and all the incidences of warfare on other sectors of the line, and so it became more a question of degree, but after our trip to the Somme I realised what a truly demoralising affect mere mud could have.*[9]

1. Miles, W. Military Operations France and Belgium 1916 Vol 2 (Macmillan and Co 1938) p.373.
2. Dudley Ward, C.H. The 56th Division (John Murray 1921) p.79.
3. Captain T.A .McLellan, 9th Argyll & Sutherland Highlanders attached 1/14th Londons, KIA 25.9.16. Buried Delville Wood Cemetery.
4. 2/Lt (Acting Captain) A.C. Wilson MC, 1/14th Londons, KIA 25.9.16. Buried Bronfay Farm Military Cemetery.
5. Grey, W.E. The 2nd City Of London Regiment (Royal Fusiliers) in the Great War 1914-19 (The Regiment 1929) p.142-143.
6. 168th Brigade War Diary PRO WO95/2951.
7. Miles op cit. p.390.
8. Dudley Ward op cit. p.96.
9. Stuart Dolden, A. Cannon Fodder: An Infantryman's Life on the Western Front 1914-18 (Blandford Press 1988) p.91.

Chapter Six

A GUIDE TO THE COMBLES
BATTLEFIELD TODAY

1. Touring Combles by Car

*This tour will take around three hours, depending on how much time you spend at a given location, and could easily be fitted into a more general tour of the Somme area, perhaps in conjunction with suggested tours in other **Battleground Europe** publications. Due to the nature of some of the local roads there is a certain degree of walking involved, although this is optional. Information on the cemeteries mentioned can be found in Chapter 7.*

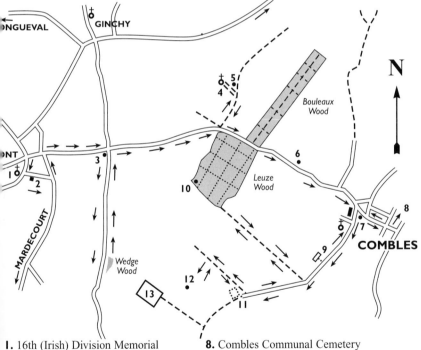

1. 16th (Irish) Division Memorial
2. German Bunkers
3. 20th (Light) Division Memorial
4. Original site of Dickens Cross
5. Dickens Cross
6. Water tower
7. War memorial

8. Combles Communal Cemetery
9. Guards Cemetery, Combles
10. German Bunker
11. Modern Falfemont Farm
12. Field Grave
13. Site of original Falfemont Farm

➡ **Car Tour Route**

Begin the tour at **Guillemont**. Park your car outside the church. This village was behind the German lines when the Battle of the Somme began, but following the capture of the nearby Trones Wood on 13th/14th July 1916, it became the next objective. However, Guillemont was flanked to the north by Waterlot Farm, to the west by a quarry which afforded good views across to the British positions at Trones Wood, and to the south a sunken lane. For the next two months the fighting here revolved around these three locations, turning the battlefield into a vast lunar-landscape of shell holes. Guillemont itself was shattered beyond recognition. Finally captured by elements of the 20th (Light) Division in September 1916, the Guards Division was here during the fighting for Ginchy. While 56th (London) Division was in action near Combles, Guillemont was the area of operations of 16th (Irish) Division whose **Divisional Memorial** you can now see outside Guillemont Church.

Leaving the church go south on the D64, and as the road bends just before the outskirts of the village, there is a road to your left. Take this road, and stop alongside a fenced-off field on your right, after about 50 yards. In this field are several **German bunker** entrances. This bunker, which consists of two main chambers, was constructed in 1915. It seems initially to have been used by German artillery units as a munitions depot and then headquarters. During the fighting for Guillemont it was no doubt used as a German regimental HQ, and once the village was in British hands it was used in a similar fashion. Indeed,

The road junction east of Guillemont, looking out towards the Quadrilateral.

the walls do have British graffiti on them. The bunkers are on private land and cannot be visited without permission of the owner. Contact the mayor of Guillemont, Monsieur Dazin, via the Mairie.

Stay on this road until you reach a T-junction. Here turn left. At the end turn right onto the D20 and continue out of the village until you reach a cross-roads with a memorial on the right-hand corner.

This is the **20th (Light) Division Memorial**. It was once a tall column, erected by the divisional Old Comrades Association in the early 1920s. Another was erected at Langemarck, in the Ypres Salient, to commemorate the Division's action there in 1917. By the early 1990s the memorial was showing signs of age, and it was found that the central column was in such a poor condition that it would have to be demolished. Funds were raised to replace the memorial, but there was not enough to return it to its former glory. Instead the current compromise was the replacement memorial; a stone slab incorporating the original bronze plaque and wreath.

From here there are fine views towards the Combles battlefield. To the left of the road, in the distance, is Bouleaux Wood. Towards the wood, and again left of the road, you should just be able to pick out the memorial cross to Major C.C.Dickens. It was in this area that the 1/4th Londons, Rangers and London Scottish fought alongside the 16th (Irish) Division in the capture of Ginchy (the village immediately to your left at the end of the road). Ahead is Leuze Wood, and the ground fought over in the early battles for Combles. To the right are the tree-tops of Wedge Wood and what the French now call 'Bois de Faffémont'. This was the location of Falfemont Farm, captured by the Dorsets of 5th Division. The village away to your far right is Maurepas, in the French sector, where their attacks on Combles were launched from. To your right rear is Hardecourt-aux-Bois, a reserve area for the 56th (London) Division during the fighting.

At the cross-roads turn right on a minor road going south. It can be muddy in the winter months, and difficult to negotiate, although it is a metalled road. Continue into the valley until you reach a small wood on the left. Stop. This is **Wedge Wood**, and here you will see the nature of the ground and how the folds were able to shield the troops who fought here from the Germans at Leuze Wood and Combles. Wedge Wood was usually the location of the battalion reserve, battalion headquarters, and occasionally brigade headquarters as well. There are signs of shell holes amongst the trees, and in recent years the wood has been used as a dumping ground for live shells. These should be left alone, as they are still fatal even after more than 85 years in the ground.

Bouleaux Wood from the Combles road, looking towards the location of Victoria Trench.

The main street of Combles then and now.

Return to the cross-roads and turn right on the D20 and continue until the road bends to the right. On this bend, on the left, is a sign post for the **Memorial to Captain C.C.Dickens**. This is reached by a track. This is passable for cars in the summer months, but is often water-logged in the wet season. It is therefore wise to park your car at the bottom of the lane and walk up. The cross is reached after a short walk of around ten minutes. This memorial was once at the end of a long, narrow copse which was located to the left of this track. It was where Jack Tucker and his comrades of the Kensingtons (see Chapter 2) properly buried Major Dickens when they returned to the area later on in 1917. After the war the ground was acquired by the Dickens family, and by the 1980s the memorial was dwarfed by a wild thicket. Tom Fairgrieve of the CWGC at Delville Wood used to keep an eye on it, but it was clear that a more permanent solution would have to be sought. In the 1990s, in conjunction with the Western Front Association and the Dickens family, the memorial was moved and the area of the copse returned to the farmer. A final search for the grave of Major Dickens was made, but nothing was found. Because of this his name was added to the Addenda panel of the Thiepval Memorial. The commune of Ginchy is now responsible for the upkeep of this

memorial. From here you also have a good view across to **Bouleaux Wood**, and the actions described in the previous chapters.

Return to your car and/or the road, and turn left on the D20. Pass **Leuze Wood** on your right, and Bouleaux Wood on the left. Both are private property and cannot be entered from here. Continue on the D20 and go into Combles. As you reach the heart of the village, you will see the large Mairie-Ecole on the right. There is parking opposite, in view of the modern church. Stop here.

This was the location of **Combles Church** before the Great War. It was just a pile of rubble by 1918, and could not be rebuilt on the original site - the new one is seen nearby. Below it and close by were some of the entrances to the catacombs described by Ernst Jünger in Chapter 1. Just below the parking area is the village **War Memorial**. The entrance to the tunnels

Combles Communal Cemetery Extension.

remained open here until after the war, but has now been closed up. Recent plans to reopen the tunnels have currently (2001) come to nothing.

In the village follow the signs for Peronne, pass the main shops and entrance to the private camp site. The road bends sharply to the right here and climbs up a hill until it reaches a cross-roads. Here go left and follow the CWGC signs for Combles Communal Cemetery Extension.

Combles Communal Cemetery Extension is the main Combles cemetery and contains graves from the fighting here in 1916. It was greatly expanded after the war, when small cemeteries on the battlefield near Bouleaux and Leuze Woods were closed and moved here. A single war grave is also found in the attached French civilian cemetery.

Return to the Mairie-Ecole in the village and here follow the CWGC signs for Guards Cemetery, along a road to the left of the modern church. Continue out of the village along this narrow minor road until you reach the cemetery on the right. Park at the bottom and walk up.

Guards Cemetery, Combles, was not made until the end of 1916 by units of the Guards Division, who were here during the winter of 1916/17. There are no London graves from the September fighting. However, there are good views across the fields to Leuze Wood and Falfemont Farm.

Return to your car. You can now take an optional walking route. This

118

vill last about 45 minutes. Stay on the minor road and follow it past a wayside shrine. A track appears on the right, and follow this uphill to **Leuze Wood**. At the end, where it meets the wood, look back and you have an excellent view over this part of the battlefield. Using the trench maps contained elsewhere in the book you can locate the area of The Loop, the tank action on 15th September, and there is a good view towards Falfemont Farm. The wood itself is private, but if you follow the edge around the south-west face you will see signs of trenches and shell holes. On the tip of the western corner of the wood is a **German Bunker**. It has a **modern memorial** to a London Regiment officer on it.

Return via the edge of the wood to the track and retrace your steps to the car. Continue in your car until you reach the modern Falfemont Farm (the French call it Ferme de Faffémont). Park on a corner alongside one entrance to the farm, remembering to leave plenty of room for other vehicles. The next stage of the tour is on foot. Leaving your car, take the track going north-west from this corner of the farm. The dogs will probably bark as you go by as there are few visitors to this area! However, they normally stay in the confines of the house. Take some dog biscuits with you if you are worried! Stay on this track as it climbs uphill. After about two hundred yards turn sharp left and go straight across the field. There was once another track here, but it has been ploughed up. Take care not to damage crops as you cross the field, but do not fear any recriminations by the farmer as you are following a legitimate route to a designated war grave.

Eventually you will find the **Field Grave** of Captain Richard Heumann, CSM Bertie Mills and Sgt Torrance. The circumstances of their death are described in Chapter 2. Despite its isolated location, the

Entrance to the modern Falfemont Farm. Beware of the dogs!

grave is still tended by the CWGC and remains in good condition. From here there are excellent views up towards Leuze Wood, and an appreciation of the ground and how difficult it was to attack The Loop can be had from this location as well. To the north-west are the trees showing the location of the original Falfemont Farm, which can be explored if you have the time and/or the energy. Return via the same route to **Falfemont Farm** and your car.

This is the last stop on the Car Tour. There are possible **follow up visits** to the cemeteries mentioned in Chapter 7, or the Thiepval Memorial where most of those who died at Combles are commemorated. Delville Wood is only about fifteen minutes away in the car from Combles, where you can get hot and cold drinks, light snacks and ice-cream in the summer. The whole range of *Battleground Europe* books are also on sale here, as are many other publications, reproduction trench maps, militaria, postcards and medals. Jane Fairgrieve is always on hand to give you a friendly welcome, and her husband, Tom, is now the curator of the South African Museum in the wood - which is well worth a visit. Both the museum and shop are closed on Mondays, and there are varying opening hours between the summer and winter months.

2. Walking The Combles Battlefield

Like most locations on the Somme, the area around Combles is ideally suited for a walking tour, with many quiet roads and farm tracks. The battlefield has been split into three walks, each looking at a different part of the fighting or landscape around Combles. Locations named in bold text refer either to locations already described in the Car Tour (above) or a cemetery/memorial described in Chapter 7.

WALK 1:
GUILLEMONT - COMBLES - LEUZE WOOD
(Duration: approximately 3 hours)

Park your car alongside the church in **Guillemont**. From the church follow the road south on the D64, and as the road bends just before the outskirts of the village, there is a road to your left. Take this road, and stop alongside a fenced off field on your right after about 50 yards. In this field are several **German Bunker** entrances. At the end turn left into a minor road. Turn right onto the D20, and continue until you reach a cross-roads. This is the **20th (Light) Division Memorial**, and from here there are spectacular views across the battlefield. To the left

The evocative Guards Cemetery, Combles.

of the road, in the distance, is Bouleaux Wood. Towards the wood, and again left of the road, you should just be able to pick out the memorial cross to Major C.C.Dickens. It was in this area that the 1/4th Londons, Rangers and the London Scottish fought alongside the 16th (Irish) Division in the capture of Ginchy (the village immediately to your left at the end of the road). Ahead is Leuze Wood, and the ground fought over in the early battles for Combles. To the right are the tree-tops of Wedge Wood and what the French now call 'Bois de Faffémont'. This was the location of Falfemont Farm, captured by the Dorsets of 5th Division. The village away to your far right is Maurepas, in the French sector, where their attacks on Combles were launched from. To your right rear is Hardecourt-aux-Bois, a reserve area for the 56th (London) Division during the fighting.

At the memorial turn right on a minor road going south. This will lead you to **Wedge Wood**. From here continue on the road for a little way, and past the quarry cut across the ground on the left and go across the fields to the small wood that now marks the spot of the original **Falfemont Farm**. As you cross the fields respect the crops that are growing in them. Follow the track round the edge of this wood (Bois de Faffémont) and follow it for a hundred yards or so. Then turn sharp left and go across the fields to the Field Grave of Captain Richard Heumann, CSM Bertie Mills and Sgt Torrance. This is a legitimate, and the only, route to what is a designated war grave. From here there are good views up to Leuze Wood and across to Combles. On the other side of the field grave, continue across the field until you meet another track. Here go right downhill until you reach the modern farm. Now take the metalled road until you reach the entrance to **Guards**

Cemetery on your left. Visit the cemetery and then backtrack towards the farm. There is a track on your right. Follow this uphill until you reach the edge of **Leuze Wood**. From here there are good views to Combles, the site of The Loop and the tank action on 15th September.

Continue around the south-west face of Leuze Wood. Among the trees you will see signs of trenches and shell holes. On the tip of the western corner of the wood is a **German Bunker**. It has a **modern memorial** to a London Regiment officer on it. Continue around the edge of the wood, where you will soon join a track. Follow this to the D20 main road. From here there are good views across the northern part of the battlefield around Bouleaux Wood and towards Ginchy.

From here you can make an optional visit to the **Memorial to Major C.C. Dickens** by following the signposted track opposite until you reach the memorial cross. There are good views of **Bouleaux Wood** from there. Otherwise continue along the D20, returning to the church at Guillemont and your car.

WALK 2:
GINCHY - QUADRILATERAL - BOULEAUX WOOD - LEUZE WOOD
(Duration: approximately 2¹/₂ hours)

Park your car by the church in Ginchy. Go south on the main road in the village, and then left at the cross-roads following signs for LesBoeufs and Morval. Continue out of the village and, where the road forks, take the right-hand road signposted for Morval. Stay on this straight section of road until you meet a bend. Stop.

Here you are on the site of the **Quadrilateral**. This German position was a thorn in the side of the Guards, 16th (Irish) and 56th (London) Divisions in September 1916. The Guards Memorial can be seen just to the north from here. To the south there are good views across the battlefield towards **Bouleaux Wood**, the Memorial to Major C.C.Dickens and the ground fought over in early-mid September 1916. Continue along the Morval Road into the Vallée du Marécage (as it is marked on modern French maps). Here take a track going south-west, which links with another running roughly in parallel to Bouleaux Wood. Continue until you reach the **Memorial to Major C.C.Dickens**.

From the memorial continue along the track to the D20. Here it meets the northern corner of Leuze Wood. Here follow a track running parallel to the wood, and then along the edge of the tree-line to the tip of the western corner of the wood. Here there is a **German Bunker**. It

One of a number of information panels placed on the battlefield by the Historial museum at Peronne, and the Somme Tourist Office. This one is close to the Combles war memorial.

...as a **modern memorial** to a London Regiment officer on it.

Return to the D20 and follow towards Guillemont. At the cross-roads stop at the **20th (Light) Division Memorial**. From here you have excellent views back across the battlefield. Take the road going north from the memorial, back to Ginchy church and your car.

WALK 3:
COMBLES - BOULEAUX WOOD - COMBLES
(Duration: approximately 2¹/₂ hours)

Park your car at **Combles Communal Cemetery Extension**. This is the main Combles cemetery and contains graves from the fighting here in 1916. A single war grave is also found in the attached French civilian cemetery. From the cemetery follow the road (D20) back into the village, making your way to the large Mairie-Ecole. Before you reach here you will see the village **War Memorial**.

Behind it and above was the location of **Combles Church** before the Great War; just a pile of rubble by 1918. It could not be rebuilt on the original site – the new one is seen nearby. Directly behind was one of the entrances to the catacombs described by Ernst Jünger in Chapter 1. The entrance to the tunnels remained open here until after the war, but has now been closed up. Recent plans to reopen the tunnels have currently (2001) come to nothing.

Stay on the D20 and follow it in the direction of Guillemont and out of the village. As it leaves Combles, the road becomes sunken. This was the sunken road that featured heavily in the final attacks. On the right you reach a water tower up on the high embankment. There is an access track here; follow it to the top. There are good views across the battlefield towards both Bouleaux Wood and Leuze Wood from here. Return to the road (D20) and continue. You will soon pass through the two woods, and a little further on is a sign posted track leading to the **Memorial to Major C.C.Dickens**. This is reached by following the track. Pass the memorial and continue along the track to where it meets the Morval road. Go right in the direction of Morval and, at a small chapel on the right, follow a track across the fields to where it meets another. Here turn right and go south. From here there are good views towards **Bouleaux Wood**.

This track meets another and takes you back into Combles and on to the D20. Follow the D20 back through the village (perhaps stopping at one of the cafés en-route!) and return to the cemetery and your car.

Chapter Seven

CEMETERIES AND MEMORIALS CONNECTED WITH THE FIGHTING AT COMBLES

There are a number of cemeteries connected with the fighting at Combles in September 1916, several of which formed part of the visits outlined in the previous chapters. For ease of reference they are outlined here in this gazetteer. They are listed in order of distance from Combles, with the nearest ones first. Only cemeteries where there are a significant number of London Regiment commemorations are listed. Details of the Thiepval Memorial are also included, as this is where the 'missing' from the actions at Combles are commemorated.

Combles Communal Cemetery Extension
Guards Cemetery, Combles
Guillemont Road Cemetery
Delville Wood Cemetery, Longueval
London Cemetery and Extension, High Wood
Bronfay Farm Military Cemetery
Grove Town Cemetery, Méaulte
Bray Military Cemetery
Thiepval Memorial

COMBLES COMMUNAL CEMETERY EXTENSION

Combles Communal Cemetery was used by the Germans for military burials from 1915 onwards, when a Bavarian Field Ambulance operated here. A British soldier of 2nd Manchester Regiment taken prisoner in August 1915, and who died of his wounds, was buried in the cemetery at that time. Following the capture of Combles, an Extension was started in October 1916 by French troops and 94 soldiers were buried here (they have since been removed to French cemeteries). By December 1916 several British units were holding the line near Rancourt and buried their dead in the cemetery. In March 1917, following the German withdrawal to the Hindenburg Line, the Extension was no longer used. It was reopened more than a year later in June 1918, when Combles was once again behind German lines. At this time 194 German soldiers were buried in the Extension in what was afterwards Plot I of the post-war cemetery. When the 18th

The impressive entrance to Combles Communal Cemetery Extension.

(Eastern) Division recaptured Priez Farm and the Combles area in August 1918 further burials were made. However, in the early 1920s Plots II, V, VI and VII were made by the concentration of 944 graves from the surrounding area. The principal cemeteries from which these men came were:

FRÉGICOURT COMMUNAL CEMETERY: where four British soldiers were buried in the winter of 1916-17.

LEUZE WOOD CEMETERY, COMBLES

Located in the north-east corner of the wood, it contained the graves of eleven British and five French soldiers who fell between September 1916 and January 1917. The French were moved to another location – possibly the French National Cemetery at Rancourt.

LONGTREE DUMP MILITARY CEMETERY, SAILLY-SAILLISEL

South of the Morval-Sailly road, there were twenty French and twelve British burials here from the December 1916 to February 1917 period. Again the French were removed to another location.

MAUREPAS MILITARY CEMETERY

On the south-west side of the village, there were twelve French, nine British and one German prisoner here. All died between

December 1916 and February 1917. The French were removed to the Maurepas French National Cemetery.

Combles Communal Cemetery Extension contains the graves of 1,041 British soldiers (the Germans were also removed), five Canadians and one South African. The unnamed graves amount to 616, over half the total, and there are Special Memorials to nine British and one South African soldiers. Other Special Memorials commemorate those once buried in Longtree Dump and Maurepas Cemeteries whose graves were destroyed by shell fire in 1918.

The graves from the Combles fighting are dominated by a group of Middlesex Regiment burials, among them the officers who fell in the fighting on 15th September 1916. Nearby is one of the tank crew of tank C14, Cpl G.E. Pattinson (VII-A-21). Captain M.M. Webb (VII-G-

Corporal Pattinson, one of the crew of tank C14, buried in Combles Communal Cemetery Extension.

19) can also be found here: it was said of him that he was 'an outstanding example of the many young officers who fulfilled responsibilities of command far beyond their years, and yet retained all the high spirits and light-heartedness of youth.' From Hatch End, Middlesex, Webb was only 24 years old.

GUARDS CEMETERY, COMBLES

The cemetery was started by the Guards Division during the winter of 1916/17, when they were holding the line beyond Combles. Other units, most notably the 29th Division, also added burials at this time. The cemetery was not used after March 1917, but a few were added in March, August and September of 1918. By this time there were 100 graves, of which 19 were men from Guards units. Plot II was added after the war when 56 burials were moved from Priez Farm – largely from units in the 18th (Eastern) and 58th (London) Divisions. Six

The author's daughter, Poppy, opening the small bronze locker contained in every CWGC cemetery. Here will be found the visitors' book and cemetery register, giving further information on those buried here.

German graves were removed in the 1920s. Some British graves from Combles German Cemetery (closed in the 1920s) were also moved here.

Guards Cemetery, Combles, one of three Western Front cemeteries bearing this proud name, has 152 British burials, four Newfoundland and fifteen unidentified. There are 30 Special Memorials to men once buried in Priez Farm and Combles German Cemetery whose graves were destroyed in 1918.

There are no 56th (London) Division burials here from the fighting at Bouleaux and Leuze Woods: the cemetery did not exist then. Most of those buried here died in quiet periods in the line between Combles, Rancourt and Sailly-Saillisel. Among the 29th Division burials are two brave officers. Major Guy Horsman Baily MC (I-D-1) of L Battery Royal Horse Artillery, was killed on 28th February 1917, aged 25. He was a veteran of the Gallipoli campaign where he had been awarded the Military Cross for 'coolness under fire'. Lieutenant Colonel A.J.H.Bowen DSO & Bar (I-D-8) was killed commanding 2nd Monmouthshires (the divisional pioneers) 2nd March 1917, aged 31. Bowen had been in France since 1914, and was decorated twice for bravery. Previously he had served with the 4th South Wales Borderers since 1908. He was killed whilst personally supervising the construction of a new trench near Sailly-Saillisel.

GUILLEMONT ROAD CEMETERY

Guillemont Road Cemetery was started by Field Ambulances of the RAMC in September 1916 and dealt with casualties at Guillemont, near Ginchy and the fighting for Combles. The original graves (121

Delville Wood Cemetery in the early 1920s.

burials) from this period are in Plot I, to the left of the main entrance. After the war the cemetery was enlarged by the concentration of graves from the surrounding area and total commemorations are now: 2,251 British, 1 Canadian, 1 Australian, 1 South African, 1 Newfoundland and 3 Germans. The unidentified number 1,523 and there are Special Memorials to 8 British soldiers.

Most visitors to this cemetery come to see Lieutenant Raymond Asquith (I-B-3), the son of the then Prime Minster, who was killed with 3rd Grenadier Guards on 15th September 1916. In the same row is his young cousin, the poet Lieutenant Hon. Edward Wyndham Tennant (I-B-18), who fell with 4th Grenadier Guards a week later on the 22nd. Plot I also contains some men from the 56th (London) Division, among them Major G.A.Stacey DSO (I-D-1), who had survived Leuze Wood in September, only to be killed on 9th October 1916 near LesBoeufs. A cousin of the commanding officer, Lieutenant Colonel Attenborough, Stacey had been an officer with the 2nd Londons since 1902 and had won the DSO for bravery in 1915. In addition, he had been Mentioned in Dispatches and awarded the Legion of Honour.

Elsewhere in the cemetery are men from both the 5th and 56th (London) Divisions killed near Combles and the Woods, among them some of the London Scottish killed in the fighting close to the Quadrilateral on 10th September 1916.

The only cemetery of note moved in here was:

HARDECOURT FRENCH MILITARY CEMETERY
In September 1916 the Artillery of 56th (London) Division buried five gunners here among the French graves from the July-September fighting. In 1918 the village was retaken by the 12th (Eastern) Division, who made another sixteen burials of the 9th Royal Fusiliers and 7th Royal Sussex.

DELVILLE WOOD CEMETERY, LONGUEVAL
Delville Wood was the scene of terrific fighting involving, amongst others, the 1st South African Brigade of 9th (Scottish) Division from 14th July 1916. Following their action, parts of the wood changed hands on an almost daily basis and many other battalions, brigades and divisions came into what the soldiers came to call 'Devil's Wood'. Fought over again in March and August 1918, the South Africans purchased the wood after the war and placed a National Memorial to their war dead here. In the 1980s a Museum was added, and there is

also a Visitors Centre and Bookshop.

The cemetery was made after the Armistice by the concentration of a few small cemeteries and of isolated graves (almost all of July, August and September, 1916) from the Somme battlefields. There are over 5,500 casualties commemorated here. Of these, nearly two-thirds are unidentified and Special Memorials are erected to 26 soldiers from the United Kingdom and one from South Africa, known or believed to be buried among them. Other special memorials record the names of three soldiers from the United Kingdom, buried in Courcelette Communal Cemetery German Extension, whose graves were destroyed by shell fire. Fifteen French graves have been removed to another cemetery. Of the total there are 5,236 British, 152 South African, 81 Australian, 29 Canadian, 19 New Zealand and 3 whose unit could not be identified.

Among the cemeteries from which British graves were concentrated into Delville Wood Cemetery are the following:

ANGLE WOOD CEMETERY, GINCHY, was a group of graves in an "excavated shell-hole" in Angle Wood, to the north-west of Maurepas; and in them were buried 27 soldiers from the United Kingdom (mainly of the London Regiment) who fell in August and September, 1916.

BATTERY COPSE CEMETERY, CURLU (called by the French Bois Vieux No. 2 Mixed Cemetery), was between Curlu and Maurepas. It contained, in addition to French graves, those of 17 soldiers from the United Kingdom who fell in 1916-18.

BAZENTIN-LE-PETIT GERMAN CEMETERY was at the south-east end of the village; it contained the graves of 2,178 German soldiers, one French, and five (who fell in March and April, 1918) from the United Kingdom.

COURCELETTE COMMUNAL CEMETERY GERMAN EXTENSION contained the graves of three soldiers from the United Kingdom, one from Canada, and 1,040 German.

FERME-ROUGE FRENCH MILITARY CEMETERY, CURLU (called by the French Bois-Vieux "B" Cemetery), was close to Battery Copse Cemetery. It contained 138 French graves and that of one soldier from the United Kingdom who fell in March, 1917.

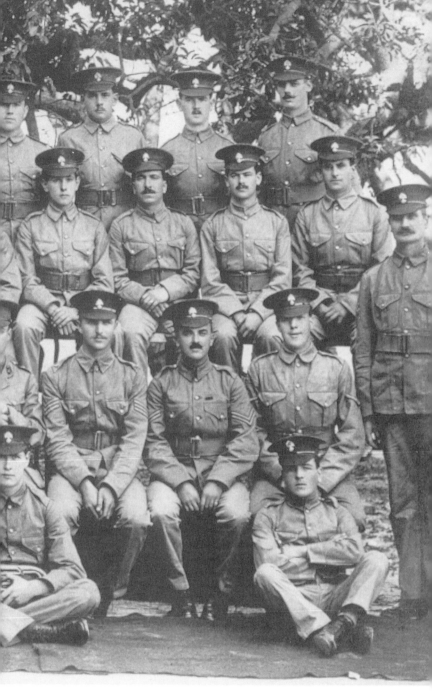

Soldiers of the 1/2nd Londons in Malta. L/Cpl Harry Woodfield, who fell at Leuze Wood, is in the centre of the rear row. (Tony Swift)

GUILLEMONT GERMAN CEMETERY No. 1, at the west end of the village, containing 221 German graves and those of seven soldiers from the United Kingdom who fell in May and July, 1918.

LONE RIDGE CEMETERY, LONGUEVAL, between Delville Wood and the centre of the village, contained the graves of 52 soldiers of the 38th (Welsh) Division and the 6th Dragoon Guards who fell at the end of August, 1918.

MARICOURT (DE LA COTE) GERMAN CEMETERY, on the south west side of the village, contained the graves of five soldiers and airmen from the United Kingdom.

MARTINPUICH GERMAN CEMETERY No. 1, at the north-east end of the village, contained the graves of six soldiers and one sailor from the United Kingdom who fell in March 1918.

MARTINPUICH GERMAN CEMETERY No. 2, 365 metres West of No. 1, contained the grave of one soldier from the United Kingdom.

Of the men from the fighting for Combles and the 56th (London) Division buried here, the majority come from the area west of Bouleaux Wood. Many of these would have been isolated graves or shell hole burials. There are a few from the Falfemont Farm area, including most of the officers of the 1st Norfolks who fell in the capture of the farm.

LONDON CEMETERY AND EXTENSION, HIGH WOOD

London Cemetery was originally started by units of the 47th (2nd London) Division after their capture of High Wood on 15th September 1916. Alongside the road from Martinpuich to Longueval they buried a large number of London Regiment men in a series of shell holes. This cemetery was made permanent in the early 1920s, but by this time more and more bodies were being found on the battlefields as buildings were erected, roads widened and fields and woods cleared. The then Imperial War Graves Commission was in need of large concentration cemeteries to place these burials, and on the Somme (although strictly speaking it is in the Pas de Calais) Serre Road No 2 Cemetery was initially selected. This site rapidly began to fill up from the battlefields north of the Ancre, and so another site were needed. The Commission then decided to expand the London Cemetery and in the late 1920s burials were started in the Extension. These Great War burials continued until after the Second World War, when, in 1946, 165 1939-45 graves were also moved here. The commemorations now total 3,874, plus 101 in the original cemetery.

The majority of the burials here are unknowns, and although research shows there are soldiers killed at Combles buried in the cemetery, it is not possible to individually identify most of them. One exception is Lance Corporal Harry Woodfield of 1/2nd Londons (Royal Fusiliers). Woodfield was killed near Leuze Wood on 17th September 1916 and posted missing. With no further news of him, the War Office concluded that he was killed on that date and his name would be added to the Thiepval Memorial. However, in 1938 a local farmer found his body near the site of The Loop and he was subsequently buried in Plot X, Row C, Grave 20.

BRONFAY FARM MILITARY CEMETERY

Bronfay Farm was a large farm complex south of Maricourt which served as a headquarters and Advanced Dressing Station (ADS) for troops in the line in this sector of the Somme battlefield. The French had started burials here in October 1914, and it was used by British troops from August 1915 until February 1917. As the battle progressed additional medical personnel were brought in and XIV Corps Main Dressing Station was opened in the summer of 1916. A few burials were made in 1918, and after the war 42 burials were moved in from the area between Bronfay Farm and Bray-sur-Somme.

Buried at Bronfay Farm are: 516 British soldiers, 15 Australian, 2 Indian, 1 South African and 1 whose unit is not known. There are 13 unnamed graves and 2 Special Memorials to British soldiers believed to be buried amongst them.

There are only a few Combles casualties in this cemetery, but amongst them is Lieutenant D.L.Child (I-C-37) of 1/2nd Londons who died of wounds on 11th September 1916. He was a member of Captain Heumanns O-Group which was wiped out in the shell-hole close to Falfemont Farm. Originally a member of the 2/2nd Londons, he had served with them at Gallipoli.

GROVE TOWN CEMETERY, MÉAULTE

Méaulte is the next village and commune below Albert, and on the left bank of the River Ancre. Grove Town Cemetery is about three miles from Albert, and in the fields outside the village. In September 1916 the 34th and 2/2nd London Casualty Clearing Stations RAMC were established at this point (called locally "la demie-lieue," and by the British, 'Grove Town'), to deal with casualties from the Somme battlefields. They were moved to the Arras front in April 1917 and, except for a few burials in August and September 1918, the cemetery was closed. Total burials are: 1,366 soldiers from the United Kingdom, 14 from Australia, 11 from Newfoundland, 1 from New Zealand, 1 French soldier, and 34 German prisoners. The cemetery stands on high ground overlooking Bray and the Somme valley.

There are few Combles casualties buried here, but a veteran of the fighting at Leuze Wood who died in later fighting is buried in this cemetery and is worthy of note: war poet Sergeant Leslie Coulson (I-J-24). Frederick Leslie A. Coulson was born at Hendon in 1889. Unlike most of the war poets, he was not from a privileged background and worked as a journalist in the years before the war, following in the footsteps of his father. He was a Reuters correspondent by 1914. When war came he joined the 2/2nd London Regiment (Royal Fusiliers) in September 1914, and went with them to Malta and Gallipoli, where he first saw action. The 2/2nd Londons were disbanded in early 1916 and he was transferred to the 1/12th Londons (The Rangers) in France. He served with them at Combles, Leuze ('Lousy) Wood until wounded near Le Transloy Ridge on 7th October, dying of his wounds at a Casualty Clearing Station at Grove Town, Méaulte, the following day. Like many of the War Poet generation, his reputation came about after his death in France, his only volume of poetry being published posthumously in 1917 under the title, *From An Outpost and other Poems*.

BRAY MILITARY CEMETERY

Bray Military Cemetery was started in April 1916 by fighting units and Field Ambulances serving in the line between Mametz and Maricourt. In September, 1916, the front line having been pushed further east, it was used by the XIV Corps Main Dressing Station; and in 1917 the 5th, 38th and 48th Casualty Clearing Stations RAMC came forward and used it. In March 1918, the village and the cemetery fell into German hands; but the village was retaken by Australians in August, when the cemetery was used once again. After the Armistice 97 graves were brought into Plot I, Rows A and B, and Plot II, Rows J and K, from the battlefields immediately north and south of the village. In 1924 106 further isolated graves were brought in and buried in Plot III.

The burials here total: 739 British, 31 Australian, 9 Indian Labour Corps, 8 Egyptian Labour Corps, 4 Indian Army, 3 Canadian, 2 South

African and 79 whose unit is unknown. There are 127 unnamed graves.

There are not many soldiers from the Combles fighting here, but they include Second Lieutenant E.H.Collcutt (III-C-25) of 1/8th Middlesex Regiment. He died of wounds received near Bouleaux Wood on 11th September 1916, aged 34.

THIEPVAL MEMORIAL
'The Missing of the Somme'

Of the 150,000 British soldiers who died on the Somme in 1916, more than 72,000 have no known grave and are commemorated on the Thiepval Memorial. Located at one of the key sites on the Somme battlefield, it was designed by Sir Edwin Lutyens and was unveiled in 1932. It remains one of the most impressive memorials on the Western Front and can be seen for miles around.

The memorial commemorates more than 72,000 soldiers who died on the Somme battlefields between July 1915 and 20th March 1918. From 21st March 1918, casualties who have no known grave are commemorated on the nearby Pozières Memorial. A high proportion of the names at Thiepval are soldiers who died on the 1st July 1916. Every regiment and corps of the British army is found here, and in addition soldiers from the Royal Naval Division and South African Brigade. Every rank from Private to Brigadier-General is recorded, and the youngest soldier to die on the Somme (Pte R.Giles, Gloucestershire Regt, age 14) is commemorated on the memorial.

The London Regiment has the greatest number of names, with 4,340 listed. The majority of these names are men who fell with the 56th (London) Division at Gommecourt and in front of Combles, around Bouleaux and Leuze Woods. In fact, because of the nature of the fighting in this sector, the heavy shell fire and smashed ground, the majority of the casualties suffered by the units mentioned in this book are commemorated here at Thiepval.

The names are listed on huge panels, mounted on sixteen piers, in regimental order and then within each regiment by rank and then name. However, the register contained in bronze lockers by the main steps is in surname order. The introduction to the register, published in the 1930s, reads,

> *A few will be found and identified as the woods are cleared, or when the remaining tracts of devastated land are brought under the plough. Many more are already buried in the larger British cemeteries of the Somme, but as unidentified. To the great majority this memorial stands for grave and headstone, and this*

register for as proud a record as that for any grave.

The vast majority of those who were killed in the fighting described in this book are commemorated here at Thiepval. The nature of the ground around Bouleaux Wood and Leuze Wood, and the approaches to Combles, meant that any soldiers killed and left in the open would be eventually obliterated by the constant shell fire. Many others, hastily buried in shell holes, would have their temporary grave markers likewise destroyed and, unless these burial sites had been officially registered, there was always the likelihood of them being lost. Some bodies were found in the late 1920s and 1930s, but many are still out there on the battlefield at Combles holding a silent vigil in the ground that they contested in 1916.

Special Memorials in Combles Communal Cemetery Extension to soldiers of the QVR who fell in the final attack on Combles.

FURTHER READING

We are fortunate that, because of the class background of many London Regiment battalions, a large number of veterans have left behind some classic accounts of the Great War. Some of these also appeared in the various London Regiment unit histories, noted in the endnotes of each chapter. Some of the better memoirs are listed together below:

Memoirs

Nobbs, G. *Englishman, Kamerad! Right of The British Line* (Heinemann 1918)

– Nobbs served as a Captain in the LRB. Blinded in Leuze Wood, this book gives the account of his capture and subsequent imprisonment as a Prisoner of War.

Smith, A. *Four Years On The Western Front* (Odhams 1922)

– Superb memoir of a soldier in the transport section of the LRB. Smith was awarded the MM and Bar for his bravery.

Tucker, J.F. *Johnny Get Your Gun: A Personal Narrative of the Somme, Ypres and Arras* (William Kimber 1978)

– The author served with the Kensingtons, and this excellent account covers from the Somme to Arras and Passchendaele.

General Works

Anon, *Soldiers Died in the Great War 1914-19* CD ROM (Naval & Military Press 1998)

– A totally searchable database of more than 600,000 soldiers who fell in the Great War. Essential for the serious student of WW1.

Giles, J. *The Somme Then and Now* (After The Battle 1986)

– This timeless book continues to inspire battlefield pilgrims old and new.

Gliddon, G. *When The Barrage Lifts* (Gliddon Books 1987)

– A topographical dictionary of the whole Somme battlefields with entries for each main location. Despite the numerous mistakes, a handy volume.

McCarthy, C. *The Somme: The Day By Day Account* (Arms & Armour Press 1993)

– Largely compiled from the 1916 Official History volumes, this is nevertheless a useful reference work which no Somme library should be without.

Middlebrook, M. & M. *The Somme Battlefields* (Viking 1991)

– Classic Somme guide which includes details of the Combles area.

Miles, W. *Military Operations France and Belgium 1916* Vol 2 (Macmillan and Co 1938)

– The all too brief second volume of the Somme Official History, now reprinted by the Imperial War Museum.

Pidgeon, T. *The Tanks At Flers* (By the author 1995)

– A superb two volume reference work, volume two made up of trench maps, detailing the involvement of tanks in the Battle of Flers-Courcelette. A chapter on those attached to the 56th Division is included.

Westlake, R. *British Battalions On The Somme* (Leo Cooper 1994)

– A summary of the movements, actions and casualties of every single British army battalion which served in the Battle of the Somme. Recommended.

INDEX

The index deliberately avoids repetitive entries such as Combles, Bouleaux Wood and Leuze Wood, which are mentioned on almost every page. Only field officers of Lieut-Col and above are listed, and there is much attention to units.

143